The Original
Maria Woodworth-Etter
Devotional

The Original
Maria Woodworth-Etter
Devotional

Larry Keefauver
General Editor

THE ORIGINAL MARIA WOODWORTH-ETTER DEVOTIONAL
Published by Creation House
Strang Communications Company
600 Rinehart Road
Lake Mary, Florida 32746
Web site: http://www.creationhouse.com

Unless otherwise noted, all Scripture quotations are from the
King James Version of the Bible.

Library of Congress Cataloging-in-Publication Data
The Original Maria Woodworth-Etter Devotional / Larry
Keefauver, general editor.
1. Devotional calendars.   2. Christian life—Pentecostal
authors.
I. Keefauver, Larry.
ISBN: 0-88419-480-9
BV4811.W674 1997   242'.2—dc21   97-23287
78901234 RPG 87654321

Contents

Contents

Introduction

IN A DAY when Pentecostalism was derided and women in ministry were scorned, Maria Woodworth-Etter blazed a passionate trail across America. She held powerful evangelistic meetings in which thousands were saved and healed. Enduring the sharp criticisms of mainline religious leaders, she fearlessly listened to God's voice and helped to pioneer Pentecostalism in the early 1900s.

Born July 22, 1844, in Ohio, to parents who were not Christians, Maria did attend a Christian (Disciple) church. Her father died an alcoholic, leaving Maria's mother with eight children to raise in poverty. At the age of thirteen, she went forward in the Disciples church to accept Christ. She was not saved, however, until the next day at her baptism, when God's power so overwhelmed her that she fainted in the Spirit. She heard Jesus call her into ministry, but her church did not use women in ministry at that time in any Christian vocation except as missionaries.

She married Mr. Woodworth and they prepared to become missionaries. She suffered poverty, the death of children, and her own poor health. Maria Woodworth-Etter saw these trials as preparations for ministry. She became involved with Friends (Quakers) and for a time worshiped with them. She and her husband continued to work hard and save money for a trip west which would be her missionary outreach. She preached wherever a church would let her and raised offerings for mission work.

As she spoke one evening to a packed meeting of Disciples, the baptism of the Holy Spirit came over her. She wrote, "It seemed as if the house were full of the glory of God. I felt as if I were drawn up over the people." She preached in a place called "The Devil's Den," and revival broke out. She continued to preach revivals and started two churches. Her fiery preaching was accompanied by miracles, healings, visions, prophesies, tongues, and deliverances through the early 1900s.

These devotionals, prepared from her sermons and diary records, document her meetings through 1916. Maria Woodworth-Etter was a Spirit-baptized contemporary of William Seymour Charles Parham, Smith Wigglesworth, John G. Lake, and the Pentecostal outpouring that accompanied Azusa Street in 1906 and the subsequent years.

A forerunner of Kathryn Kuhlman, Maria Woodworth-Etter was used mightily of God to demonstrate that the power of the Holy Spirit is as real in these days as in the church of Acts. Be filled and baptized by the Spirit's power as you read and pray through these devotions.

—LARRY KEEFAUVER, D.MIN.
GENERAL EDITOR

Day 1

The Wilderness Shall Blossom

The wilderness and the solitary place shall be glad for them; and the desert shall rejoice, and blossom as the rose.

—ISAIAH 35:1

PRAISE GOD, the work is going on, and the wilderness of sin has been made to blossom as the rose! Where there was cursing and blaspheming, there is singing and praising God. Let us never be discouraged. Rather, we should lean hard on God. He will give us victory every time if we only trust Him and give Him the glory. Praise God for victory through faith in His promise and through the efficiency of the blood of the Lamb!

For the encouragement of those who are starting in the work of the Lord, let me say that God has promised to be with us always even to the end. We are nothing but the clay God speaks through. It is "Not by might . . . but by my spirit, saith the Lord of hosts" (Zech. 4:6). If the Holy Spirit is dwelling in our hearts and shining out through our lives and actions, then we, by faith, can take God at His Word. We will find at all times and places that His grace is sufficient, and He will give us victory every time.

Lord, help me to see Your potential and victory in every wilderness that I face. Amen.

Day 2

I Am Not Afraid

*Be not afraid of their faces: for I am with
thee to deliver thee, saith the Lord.*
—JEREMIAH 1:8

HE HAS SHOWN ME we are in the last days.
He has poured out his Spirit in all my
meetings. Praise God, no matter how the Holy
Ghost came, I knew the Lord was leading.
How did I realize this? It is "Not by might, nor
by power, but by my spirit, saith the Lord"
(Zech. 4:6).

When I would feel my responsible position
and look over the crowded house, I would feel
like Peter and begin to sink, crying out, "Lord,
help; Lord, use the day to thy glory, and give
me a message for this dying people."

Some of those promises would come rolling
in, accompanied with the Holy Ghost, until I
would feel lost in Christ and see nothing but
the multitude rushing on to judgment.

Oh, praise the Lord for His tender care over us and for His wonderful salvation that fills our souls with glory; that takes away the fear of persecution, the fear of man, and the fear of devils. In Christ, we can rejoice in the midst of trials, remembering that "all things work together for good to them that love God" (Rom. 8:28). Confidence in Christ takes away the fear of death. As we look at the grave, we hear a shout from Calvary saying, "I am the resurrection, and the life" (John 11:25).

> *Lord, take away all my fear so that I may only see You and not the threats all around me. Amen.*

Day 3 *8/15/08*

Conviction

And when he [the Holy Spirit] *is come,
he will reprove the world of sin, and of
righteousness, and of judgment.*
—JOHN 16:8

ONE NIGHT I was pleading with sinners to accept the invitation to be present at the marriage supper of God's only begotten Son. I felt that death was very near. I told them someone was refusing for the last time, and the coffin and winding sheet were near. Oh, how I pleaded with them to accept while there was mercy.

One old man was so convicted he could not stand it. Yet, he would not yield. He left the house, cursing the Methodist church. He thought to run away from God. But swift judgment was on his track. In going out of town the train ran over him and killed him. The next morning before seven o'clock, he was in his winding sheet and ready for the coffin.

It caused a wonderful excitement. Some said I prayed for God to kill him, and that they would not have me pray for them for fifty dollars. Others said I mesmerized the people, and many were afraid to come to the church. So I told the congregation they need not stay away. We could pray for them at their homes, and God would answer our prayers. God would make them so sin-sick that they would be glad to come to church and beg for mercy. Praise God! He was working in His own way. Conviction took hold of the people.

Lord, help me not to put off Your will for my life. Amen.

Day 4

False and Blind Teachers

For my people have committed two evils:
they have forsaken me, the fountain of
living waters, and hewed out cisterns,
broken cisterns, that can hold no water.
                              —JEREMIAH 2:13

MAY GOD HAVE MERCY on blind leaders and false teachers, and send something to arouse them before they and their followers go down to hell together. There are thousands of ministers today who are healing the "hurt of the daughter of my people slightly saying, Peace, peace;" when the Lord God says, "there is no peace" (Jer. 6:14). They are promising the people liberty, when they themselves are servants of corruption. They have left Christ, the fountain of living waters, and hewn out cisterns, broken cisterns that will not hold water. They are teaching the people the form, but denying the power. The Lord says, "Ye scornful men that rule this people . . . ye . . . have made a covenant with death, and with hell are we at agreement; . . . your covenant with death shall be disannulled, and your agreement with hell shall not stand" (Isa. 28:14–15, 18).

The people are dead in trespasses and sins, and these false teachers are making them believe they can go to heaven without being made alive to God by His Spirit in their souls. They are making them believe there is no hell and are doing away with future punishment. The Lord says they are teaching the people to hide behind a refuge of lies, but in the storm of God's wrath these refuges shall be swept away. They, with their followers, will have no hiding place. May the Spirit of God come upon every reader and cause you to search your heart in the light of God and eternity to see if you are hiding behind these refuges of lies. If so, you are on the sand. Unless you come to Christ and receive life, there is a fearful doom awaiting you.

> *Lord, I pray for my spiritual leaders that they will always speak and teach Your truth. Amen.*

Day 5

Until Jesus Returns

*Then we which are alive and remain
shall be caught up together with them in
the clouds, to meet the Lord in the air:
and so shall ever be with the Lord.*
—1 THESSALONIANS 4:17

IT IS OVER FOURTEEN years since I started out to stand between the living and the dead, to point sinners to the Lamb of God that taketh away the sins of the world. I have been going from one battlefield to another almost day and night. During this time I have travelled about 35,322 miles, and held meetings in thirteen states; have stood before hundreds of thousands. The power of the Holy Ghost has gone out from these meetings all over the United States, and been felt in many places across the mighty deep in awakening power.

I can say with Joshua, in all the promises the Lord has made, He has never failed in one, but has been with me in every trial and given grace and glory. He has conquered all my enemies and glorified His name again and again. What He has done in the past He will do in the future. I will trust Him and go forward until He calls me from labor to reward. If we as ministers, churches, and individuals, have passed through many trials and persecutions, and have borne them patiently for Christ's sake, we will in no wise lose our reward. Jesus says, "Rejoice ye in that day, and leap for joy: for, behold, great your reward is in heaven" (Luke 6:23).

Oh, what a happy meeting that will be! Whole families and friends will rise up from the old churchyards and clasp each other in a long embrace which will last forever. Parents and children shall meet, as well as husbands and wives, brothers and sisters, friends and neighbors, pastors and flocks. Those who are alive will be changed in a moment, set free from the effects of sin, and will be clothed with the glory of heaven.

> *Lord Jesus, we joyfully await Your arrival as the Bridegroom. Come quickly, Lord Jesus. Amen.*

8/18/08

Becoming God's Child

*But as many as received him, to them
gave he power to become the sons of God,
even to them that believe on his name.*

—JOHN 1:12

JESUS HAS all power. He was raised up with all power. The Holy Ghost was with the disciples, but Jesus said, "He shall be in you." When they were all together, Jesus met with them, and He opened their spiritual minds. "He breathed on them, and saith unto them, Receive ye the Holy Ghost" (John 20:22). They received Him, and became partakers of the divine nature. They received the gift of God, were enlightened, and cried out "My Lord and my God." No one ever had that experience before that time. They were sons of God by the new birth. "Yea, for the rebellious also." Eternal life is the most important of all gifts. For without this gift you can never get inside the pearly gates.

When the sinner stops his rebellion and repents, God gives him faith to accept Christ. God gives him power to become a son of God, who are born, not of man or of the will of men, or of flesh and blood, but by the power of God. He is then no longer a rebel, but a son, for he has received the gift of God and has been born of the spiritual family of God. His name has been written in the family record by the finger of God, and it has been said, "this man was born in Zion." He has the finished work on Calvary for sin and uncleanness. He is now a child of God, ready for any or all of the gifts of the Pentecostal baptism and power. He is God's man.

> *How I trust You, Jesus, for salvation!*
> *How I rejoice in being Your child.*
> *Amen.*

Day 7

Signs and Wonders

And by the hands of the apostles were many signs and wonders wrought among the people.

—ACTS 5:12

WHEN THE DISCIPLES were put into prison their lives threatened on account of God's great power within them for healing and miracles, they were forbidden to preach in the name of Jesus.

Those early Christians knew it was the power of God that caused all their persecution. They knew if they had a form of religion, and denied the power, that they would have no more trouble. But, beloved, they said, "We will be true to God. We will preach the word if we die." Then they prayed to the Lord, saying, "Lord, behold their threatenings: and grant to thy servants, that with all boldness they may speak thy word, by stretching forth thine hand to heal: and that signs and wonders may be done by the name of thy holy child Jesus" (Acts 4:29–30).

When they preached they knew they must see the signs in their meetings of the presence of the invisible Christ, who confirms His word through their message. Then, like Peter, they could say to those present, "This that you see and hear and feel, it is the promise of the Father, it is the Holy Ghost" (Acts 2:33, author's paraphrase).

The Son was pleased with their prayer and with their faith and courage. The place was shaken and they were all filled with the Holy Ghost, and spake the word with boldness (Acts 4:31).

After this event they had greater success. God did mighty signs and wonders at the hands of the apostles. Great fear fell on all the church, and on all that heard and saw these things. Multitudes of men and women came flocking to Christ.

> *Mighty Lord Jesus, confirm Your Word today with signs and wonders through the miracle-working power of Your Spirit. Amen.*

Women and Ministry

*There is neither Jew nor Greek, there is
neither bond nor free, there is neither male
nor female: for ye are all one in Christ
Jesus.*

—GALATIANS 3:28

AUL WORKED with the women in the gospel
more than any of the apostles. Priscilla
and Phoebe travelled with Paul preaching and
building up the churches (see Acts 18:2, 18, 26;
Rom. 16:1).

He and Phoebe had been holding revivals
together; but she was called to the city of
Rome. Paul could not go with her, but he was
very careful of her reputation, and to ensure
that she was treated with respect. He wrote a
letter of recommendation: "I commend unto
you Phoebe our sister, which is a servant of the
church [*servant* signified a minister of the
church] which is at Cenchrea: that ye receive
her in the Lord, as becometh saints, and that
ye assist her in whatsoever business she hath

need of you: for she has been a succorer of many, and of myself also" (Rom. 16:1–2).

Phoebe had authority to do business in the churches, and she had been successful in winning souls to Christ. Paul was not ashamed to say she had encouraged him. He spoke with the highest praise of a number of sisters who had been faithful workers in the work of the Lord, who had risked their lives in the effort to save souls; and not he alone gave them praise, but all the churches of the gentiles sent their thanks also.

Though Paul wrestled with the role of women in the church (see 1 Cor. 14:34–35; 7:1–40; 11:18), he clearly supported their ministry—and labored side by side with women. He encouraged the churches to do the same.

> *Lord Jesus, thank You for empowering women to do the faithful work of ministry within Your body of believers. Amen.*

Women Work in the Harvest

*Pray ye therefore the Lord of the Harvest,
that he will send forth labourers into his
harvest.*

—MATTHEW 9:38

MY DEAR SISTER in Christ, as you hear these words may the Spirit of God come upon you and make you willing to do the work the Lord has assigned to you. It is high time for women to let their lights shine; to bring out their talents that have been hidden away rusting, and use them for the glory of God. Let women do with their might what their hands find to do, trusting God for strength.

Oh, the fields are white, for the harvest is great and ripe, and it is ready for the gospel sickle; oh, where are the laborers to gather the golden grain into the Master's garner? The world is dying, the grave is filling, hell is boasting, and the end rapidly approaches.

* laborers work in the fields
harvesters reap

Preaching the gospel

God left the glorious work of saving souls in the hands of the church. What is the church composed of? Men, women, and children. We are putting up a building of God. Everyone has a part in this building. If we cannot be a pillar or a cornerstone, let us be a spike or a nail or a brick. Let us not despise the day of small things. Whatever we do with the right motive for Jesus is precious in His sight. God's church is a workshop; no idlers are allowed there. There should be bills posted, "To work, to work. Everyone at his post." When Satan tempts us, as he tempted Nehemiah, we should say, "I am doing a great work, so that I cannot come down. I am commissioned by the King of Heaven to work for Him" (Neh. 6:3 author's paraphrase).

"The Spirit and the bride say, Come. And let him that heareth say, Come. . . . And whosoever will, let him take the water of life freely" (Rev. 22:17).

> *Lord, inspire women to serve You in the work of Your harvest. Amen.*

Day 10

Hear the Master Calling

*But God hath chosen the foolish things of
the world to confound the wise; and God
hath chosen the weak things of the world
to confound the things which are mighty.*
— 1 CORINTHIANS 1:27

IF WE HAVE BEEN, like David, taken away
from that horrible pit over which we were
hanging by the thread of life . . .

- if our feet have been taken out of
  the mire and clay . . .
- if the chains of Satan, which were
  around us like brass and iron, have
  been broken . . .
- if our feet have been set on solid
  rock, and a new song put into our
  mouths . . .
- if we have been adopted into the
  family of God, of which part are in
  Heaven and part on earth . . .

- if our names are written in the Book of Life . . .
- Then we have the gift of eternal life—we are heirs to the bank of Heaven . . .
- to an eternal inheritance . . .
- to a mansion in the golden city . . .
- and to a robe and a crown.

Let us not plead weakness. God will use the weak things of this world for His glory. When He wanted to introduce His glorious gospel to a dying world, God did not go to the Jewish Sanhedrin and select the wise and mighty. He went along the sea of Galilee and chose twelve ignorant men and said to them, "Follow me, and I will make you fishers of men."

Oh, hear the Master calling for soldiers! He says He will lead us on to victory. Oh, who will respond to the call? Who will place his name on the heavenly roll? Who will enlist in the war and help to conquer the mighty foe? Who will help to beat back the powers of darkness?

Lord Jesus, I will follow You wherever You lead me. Amen.

Day 11

A Form of Godliness

Having a form of godliness, but denying the power thereof: from such turn away.
—2 TIMOTHY 3:15

THOSE WHO ARE OPPOSING the demonstration of the Spirit today say we do not need these things, that we are progressing with the age, that we want an intellectual religion, and that we must explain and present the Word from a human standpoint in a scientific way.

In these last days the masses of so-called religious teachers belong to the class Paul described, who have a form of godliness but deny the power (2 Tim. 3:5). From such, we must turn away. They will not endure sound doctrine and will turn the people away from the truth.

These false teachers are in a worse condition than the Jews were. They are sinning against much greater light. They are willingly blind and are teaching their followers to hide behind a refuge of lies, trusting the doctrines and traditions of men. "In vain they do worship me," saith the Lord (Matt. 15:9).

The judgments of God are coming upon the false church in the most awful way.

> *Lord, help me to worship You in Spirit and in truth, avoiding forms of godliness and the traditions of men. Amen.*

Day 12

Jesus Is Coming Quickly

*He which testifieth these things saith,
Surely, I come quickly. Amen. Even so,
come, Lord Jesus.*

—REVELATION 22:20

CHRIST WILL COME as quickly as the lightning flashes from the east to the west, and
just as quickly He will snatch His bridal company away while the world sleeps in a drunken
stupor.

But the next time He comes, all will know
it. Every knee shall bow, and every tongue
shall confess Jesus Christ as Lord (Phil.
2:10–11). Every eye shall see Him, and every
slanderous tongue will have to confess before
the world that these were God's chosen vessels.

This honor belongs to the saints. The world
will have to confess that we were right, and
that they were wrong. God is very proud of
His bride. God's children now deny themselves many of the things of the world, but

they are heirs of the kingdom even though many are poor in this world and having hard times. There is going to be a change in this old world. God is calling you to behold. Don't go a step further.

The first time the bride will be caught away. The second time she will come riding on white horses. Jesus will stand on the Mount of Olives and they that pierced Him shall see Him. You now know down in your hearts that Jesus is the Christ. God's people hear something more than natural men hear. The wisdom we get comes from God, who gives liberally to all His people. More than anything else my prayer has been, "Give me wisdom." A blind man can see if he looks with spiritual eyes at the signs of the times.

> *Lord, I am ready and waiting for the day when You will come and take Your bride. Amen.*

Day 13

The Wise Shall Shine as Stars

And they that be wise shall shine as the brightness of the firmament; and they that turn many to righteousness as the stars for ever and ever.

—DANIEL 12:3

DANIEL SAYS the wise shall know when the Lord comes. You may say, "I don't believe." You don't want to believe, but that day will overtake you as a thief in the night. None of the wicked shall understand the signs of Jesus' coming. You who are children of the light shall know, and that day will not overtake you unexpectedly.

Those who know the time of the Lord's coming shall "turn many to righteousness" and shall shine "as the stars for ever and ever."

Don't be looking to the grave. Look up— for behold, He cometh.

Lord, make us wise to discern the times. Amen.

Holy Spirit Power

*But ye shall receive power, after that the
Holy Ghost is come upon you.*

—ACTS 1:8

EARNEST INTEREST on the part of the
workers was not by any means confined
to the Stone Church people or those most
intimately connected with the work. It was
not a Stone Church affair but catholic in its
broadness.

All who came, even from a distance, threw
themselves into the work of praying with the
sick with much earnestness, showing in a
marked way the growing spirit of unity. There
was no building up of "My work," which nat-
urally characterizes individual effort, but on
every hand it was evidenced that all were
unselfishly working in the interest of Christ's
body. Missions and churches were forgotten in
the united effort to get souls to God.

God honored the faith of all, and people who had their eyes on Him received healing regardless of who prayed for them. One sick woman who came in mistook one of the sisters for Sister Etter, and asked for her prayers. The sick woman was immediately healed. We hope this will be an encouragement to some sufferers to whom Mrs. Etter cannot minister.

Healing flowed all through the church at different hours; not only in the meetings but during the day. Here and there you would see groups of people praying for the sick, and shouts of glory from the suffering ones told that the lightning from heaven had touched their bodies.

The revival, which lasted for six months and was at its flood through July, was not due to any distinctions in theology or to the setting forth of any particular doctrine or creed, but because we have been getting back to the simplicity of the gospel, and with much prayer.

Lord, manifest Your power by healing and saving all those who seek You. Amen.

*Stone Church is a local church in the Chicago area.

8/28/08

Day 15

Hindrances to Healing

But his delight is in the law of the Lord;
and in his law doth he meditate day and
night.

—PSALMS 1:2

HILE MANY PEOPLE who are prayed with
are not healed, we know that it is God's
will to heal because on the cross Jesus "took
our infirmities and bore our diseases."

We know unbelief stops God. Covenant
breakers, and those who have drawn back and
refused to walk in the light, may find that God
withholds healing until these evils are cor-
rected. Then there are those who, like Job, find
their healing delayed. They are conscious that
God's hand is on them, and a great trans-
forming work is going on in them, perfecting
patience, endurance, and victory that glorifies
God in the fire. In delay their faith may "wax
strong," their obedience be made full, and a
triumphant testimony to healing soon be

given them. God has many such witnesses.

There were many striking and wonderful miracles of healing, but there were other cases in which the healing was but partially realized. This does not disprove that a supernatural work was wrought in many at the time they were prayed for. When a soul comes to God for salvation and then goes back among his worldly associates, he is in great danger of losing his precious inheritance in Christ.

It is the same with healing. Even though there has been a mighty inflow of the resurrection life of Jesus, if the person is resting in his feelings for the validity of his healing, he goes under at the first breath of testing. Those who are not deeply grounded in the Word and are surrounded by worldly and unbelieving associates are in grave danger of backsliding from any experience they may have in God, whether salvation, healing, or the baptism.

> *Lord, help me to seek out godly people who will strengthen my faith in You. Amen.*

Day 16

Sound the Alarm

But let us, who are of the day, be sober, putting on the breastplate of faith and love: and for an helmet, the hope of salvation.

—1 THESSALONIANS 5:8

THE MAIN THING to keep before the people is the near coming of Jesus. We are not to set the day—God forbid. But the saints will know as the day draws nigh. We can tell by the signs that it is near. God expects you to preach as one having authority. This is a generation that will go up without dying. Christ looked down the age to our day and saw the whole world in unbelief, men fainting, and their hearts failing them for fear of the things that were coming upon the earth. Daniel prophesied and said the wicked should grow worse and worse, and none of the wicked should understand, but the wise shall understand.

Then the Lord gave Daniel another picture. He saw on the land and on the sea, here and there, messengers blowing trumpets, hailing each other as they passed along. For years, whenever I meet a child of God, my greeting has been, "Watchman, what of the night?" From those who have much of the Spirit of God, the answer comes, "the morning cometh." But the night is here, too. We have to preach that.

We know the darkness of hell is spreading over this earth, and it will soon be a fearful scene, a regular deluge of blood. We have to sound the alarm and give the message that the King is coming. Some will be accounted worthy to escape all these things and stand before the Son of Man.

> *Lord, help me to sound the alarm of*
> *Your coming that others may be eager*
> *to hear of Your salvation. Amen.*

3/30/08

Day 17

Why Some Go Back

For with the heart man believeth unto righteousness, and with the mouth confession is made unto salvation.

—ROMANS 10:10

THERE ARE OCCASIONALLY some who testify to healing and soon afterwards, when tempted, backslide from their healing, just as many professing conversion, and others professing the baptism, backslide. Yet we do not hear such harsh criticism concerning the latter as we do the former; all ministers and workers continue to urge men to become converted and baptized in the Spirit and warn them again backsliding. Why not do the same in reference to the healing of the body? What is wrong with this method? Did not Jesus give us to understand that all this was likely to occur, when He said, "Sin no more, lest a worse thing come upon you."

Then there may be here and there an isolated case of some enthusiast who declares he is healed and gives testimony to that effect, gladly offering to have it published, yet soon afterwards speaks of having only "taken it by faith."

And last, is it wrong to urge the person being ministered to, to act their faith by telling them to clap their hands and praise the Lord? Nay, verily, nay! I believe there can only be one answer to all the above questions, and that is, it is not wrong but is right, and therefore, these methods are encouraging faith in God with the persons being ministered to and to others desiring ministry.

> *Lord, help me to give witness with my mouth to the wondrous works You are completing in my life. Amen*

Handwritten at top: 8|31|08

Day 18

The Fire Falls

*And I, if I be lifted up from the earth,
will draw all men unto me.*

—JOHN 12:32

OR TWO YEARS Brother Foster and the saints had been calling me to Topeka to hold a convention. At last we felt that the Lord was leading, so the last of July 1915 I, with several good workers, landed in the beautiful city of Topeka.

Many of my readers have read of the great meeting we had in that city twenty-seven years ago, when I went with two young girls and a janitor as strangers, at the invitation of one minister, and held meetings for nearly two months in the beautiful park.

The dear Lord Jesus says, "If I be lifted up, I shall draw all men unto Me." He is the great drawing power. As we preached the Word, giving Him the preeminence above all men and powers, the Lord was with us, confirming the word with "signs and wonders." They began to bring the sick on beds and crutches, the lame, the blind, and the halt were seen running from their cots and beds. The blind were made to see, the lame were leaping and shouting. Sinners wept their way to Calvary, and arose praising the Lord, for they had found Him precious to their souls.

Many times the places of amusement were empty, the great theater was crowded, and many could not get in. Many ministers of different faiths came from all parts on trains, in companies, bringing the sick with them.

> *Give me the faith to believe You for a mighty move of the Holy Spirit in power upon my own life and the lives of my family, friends, and acquaintances. Amen.*

Day 19

Try the Spirits

Beloved, believe not every spirit, but try the spirits whether they are of God: because many false prophets are gone out into the world.

—1 JOHN 4:1

ELOVED, TRY THE SPIRITS." There are many spirits we do not want to have anything to do with. There is our own spirit, the flesh, and the devil. There are many spirits contending, and many times we let our own spirit rule and make ourselves think it is God; we do the same at times with the flesh and the devil.

Sometimes we know it is not God, but we want to have our own way. If we have the Holy Ghost we can prove the spirits, because everything the Holy Ghost does is confirmed by the Word. We do not want to trust tongues and interpretations. We must measure tongues and demonstrations by the Word, and if they do not agree with the Word, we must not accept them. Everything must be measured by the Word.

We do know God and the voice of God, but the devil can come as an angel of light. When you are in the Holy Ghost, that is the time the devil tries to get in and lead you astray. The Holy Ghost is revealing some secret things; at the same time the devil comes in, and if you are not careful, you will listen to what he has to say and follow him.

Once I was having a wonderful vision and right in the midst of it, the devil said to me, "You are going to die." I was very poor and was worked nearly to death. I listened to the devil for a minute. Then I stopped to hear what God wanted to teach me.

I said, "What is God showing me? Does this agree with what God is showing?" I knew I could not die if I was to give the people His message. So I listened to God and not the devil.

> *Lord, empower me to discern between*
> *Your voice and all others. Amen.*

9/2/08

Day 20

Give and God Will Give to You

Give, and it shall be given unto you . . .
For with the same measure that ye mete
withal it shall be measured to you again.
—LUKE 6:38

THE HOLY GHOST makes us level-headed. Those who stayed in the camp got as much as they who went. Be God's stewards and give the Lord His part. The cattle upon a thousand hills are His, but He works through our instrumentality. He gives you everything that you have: physical, financial, and spiritual. And He expects you to use all your powers for Him. If you give out, He will supply.

He expects you to take Him into partnership. Give Him what belongs to Him, and He will bless you. The Gospel has to be supported. Water is free, but it costs money to lay the pipes and keep the water running. Angels can fly, but men have to pay fare, and someone has to help.

If you keep the pipes in order, the gospel will be given out. You need to help with your prayers and hold up the hands of those who work. If you trust God and walk with Him, that is the work God wants of you.

Thank You, Lord, for partnering with me to spread the gospel to the world. Amen.

9|3|08

Day 21

Pentecost

*But when the Comforter is come, whom I
will send unto you from the Father, even
the Spirit of truth, which proceedeth from
the Father, he shall testify of me.*
—JOHN 15:26

HE IS THE HOLY GHOST. The Lord speaks
of the Holy Ghost as a person as much as
He would of one of the apostles. On the day
of Pentecost, they were all of one accord, in
one place, and something happened.

It will happen every day if you have the
Spirit. "Suddenly there came a sound from
heaven as of a mighty rushing wind." This was
the Holy Ghost when He came to stay. "There
appeared unto them cloven tongues like as of
fire, and it sat upon each of them. And they
were all filled with the Holy Ghost, and began
to speak with other tongues, as the Spirit gave
them utterance" (Acts 2:3–4).

When this was noised abroad, multitudes
came together. What was noised abroad? That

these people were all speaking in other languages. The news went through Jerusalem, and the multitude came together and were confounded because every man heard them speak in his own language. Those who came were men out of every nation under heaven.

They heard these hundred and twenty speak in their own language wherein they were born. This is what gathered the people and confounded them. "They were all amazed and marveled, saying one to another, Behold, are not all these which speak Galileans? And how hear we every man in our own tongue, wherein we were born? . . . we do hear them speak in our tongues the wonderful works of God" (Acts 2:7–8, 11).

> *Fire of the Holy Ghost, fall on me that I might speak in other tongues and testify of the mighty and wonderful works of God. Amen.*

Day 22

Speaking in Tongues

*And they were all filled with the Holy
Ghost, and began to speak with other
tongues, as the Spirit gave them utterance.*
—ACTS 2:4

THE HOLY GHOST is a wonderful person,
not a myth or shadow. Pentecost, when
the Holy Ghost came in to stay, is the greatest
thing that ever happened in God's work. He
came and took possession of one hundred
twenty men and women; He sat upon their
heads in cloven tongues of fire. He took possession of their bodies; then of their vocal
organs; and they spoke, everyone, as He gave
them utterance.

They spoke in languages they had never
learned, and did not know what they were
saying. The Holy Ghost took possession of
their tongues, and spoke through them; He
spoke through the clay as you would speak
through a telephone and told about Jesus. "He
shall testify of Me."

Jesus told the apostles that they should be witnesses. When the Holy Ghost came, He knew all about it, and through the apostles He told of the wonderful works of God. When this was noised abroad, multitudes gathered. It was the speaking in tongues that drew the people. When the people heard the apostles, they were confounded and said, "What meaneth this?"

I want you to notice this point—it was speaking in tongues that confounded them. The Holy Ghost spoke through these unlearned men who had never been to college to learn other languages. It was one of the most wonderful things God ever did. It is now, when God speaks through you.

Holy Spirit, take possession of my tongue. Speak through me as You did those early Christians. Amen.

Day 23

A Sign to Unbelievers

Wherefore tongues are for a sign, not to them that believe, but to them that believe not.

—1 Corinthians 14:22

GOD SENDS the Holy Ghost to come into the human body. He takes charge of the vocal organs and the person has nothing to do about it. But, for all that God does—such a wonderful thing—some of you will not believe it. Tongues are for a sign to unbelievers. In Acts, they were the worst kind of unbelievers— they had crucified the Lord. Nonetheless, they were made to believe in Jesus Christ by this sign. They were convinced by this sign that Jesus was the Messiah, when everything else had failed.

These were unlearned men, all Galileans, yet they spoke all the tongues representing the different nations in a wonderful way. It takes years and years to master other languages, and very few speak other languages fluently like natives. These were unlearned people, yet they spoke fluently, like the natives, because God Almighty spoke through them.

Everyone who is baptized in the Holy Ghost today, as he ought to be, speaks in another language, and the first words almost always are, "Jesus is coming soon!"

> *Speak through me, Holy Spirit, that*
> *unbelievers might hear Your voice and*
> *be convinced that Jesus Christ is Lord.*
> *Amen.*

Give me boldness to speak and
do, in obedience to You.

Day 24

Power From the Heart

He that believeth on me, as the scripture hath said, out of his belly shall flow rivers of living water.

—JOHN 7:38

ESUS SAID when the Holy Ghost comes in, "he shall testify of me," then you shall be witnesses. In the mouth of two or three witnesses, every word shall be established. When the Holy Ghost comes in to abide, He comes into the body like rivers of living water. The power comes from the heart, not the head. We talk through the intellect. The Holy Ghost talks through the Spirit. The Holy Ghost testifies when it is God's work.

Peter said, "This is that which was spoken by the prophet Joel" (Acts 2:16; Joel 2:28–32). "This" special thing is referring to speaking in tongues. The apostles, acting like drunken men, were talking in other languages—all this is "that spoken by the prophet." God said when His Spirit was poured out, He would speak with stammering lips and another tongue, but some will not believe it.

The cloven tongues have been seen. In Dallas and Chicago fire was seen upon the heads of some. It is the same Holy Ghost speaking in other tongues. Why not see the cloven tongues of fire?

When the Holy Ghost comes in, He will take possession of the house, take the uppermost seat, and speak Himself.

> *Lord Jesus, baptize me with Your Spirit, that out of my heart and spirit might flow living waters. Take possession of me, and speak of Yourself. Amen.*

Day 25

Speak in the Spirit

I [Paul] *thank my God, I speak with tongues more than ye all.*
—1 CORINTHIANS 14:18

PAUL DESIRED for all to speak in tongues. Yet he said that in the church he would rather speak five words with understanding that by his voice he might teach others, than ten thousand words in an unknown tongue. He urged us not to forbid one another to speak with tongues (1 Cor. 14:39).

Tongues are one of the last signs of the soon return of Jesus. For all that are baptized with the Holy Ghost, the first words they speak in an unknown tongue, when interpreted, are "Jesus is coming soon, get ready." Everyone that speaks in an unknown tongue should pray that he might interpret.

Paul said, "Desire spiritual gifts." He that speaks in an unknown tongue, speaks unto

God. No man understands him, but in the Spirit he speaketh mysteries. He edifies himself, but if he interprets or someone else interprets, he edifies the whole church.

Tongues are for a sign to unbelievers that Jesus is coming soon, and that the Holy Ghost is poured out. Those who have the gift of tongues can speak at will, or any time that the Spirit is moving. Some even lose their experience and still speak any time, anything they want to, casting reflections on the cause of Christ. Speaking in tongues without the power of the Holy Ghost is done in the flesh and is not of God.

> *God, empower me to speak by Your Spirit and not of my flesh. Amen.*

4/8/8

Day 26

Let the Spirit Work in You

And be not drunk with wine, wherein is excess; but be filled with the Spirit.
—EPHESIANS 5:18

MANY PEOPLE TEACH today that no one has the Holy Spirit until he is baptized with the Holy Ghost. The Holy Ghost comes in different degrees such as the *filling* of the Spirit, and the *baptism* in the Spirit. The baptism comes down on your head like a cloud.

When the prophets were anointed, the oil was poured over their heads, and then the Holy Ghost came into them. The Holy Ghost must come upon our heads and then all through us, taking possession of us. Many people do not think of anything but speaking in tongues. They lay everything else aside.

Thirty-five years ago I was baptized with the Holy Ghost and fire, and I stood alone. When the Pentecostal movement broke out, and some said they would not have anything but tongues, so I was kept back. I could not do much with the movement at first. There was so much false teaching that the Holy Ghost was driven away from many people. They wanted the Holy Ghost to work this way, and not that way. Let the Holy Ghost work in any way that agrees with the Word of God.

> *Holy Spirit, move in my life in whatever way You desire, that I might be Your vessel to glorify the name of Jesus. Amen.*

Day 27

Sing in the Spirit

*Praise ye the Lord. Sing unto the Lord a
new song, and his praise in the congregation of saints.*

—PSALMS 149:1

I BELIEVE THE HOLY GHOST will speak in
tongues through everyone who receives
the baptism, and you will receive the other
gifts also, if you believe for them. In these last
days, God is raising up a people who will blow
the trumpet.

How can we sing in the heavenly choir
unless we are filled with the Holy Ghost? John
heard the song of the redeemed like the
rushing of mighty waters. It is the Holy Ghost;
it rolls up and sounds like the rushing of many
waters.

We have heard the heavenly music, and
many times there are sounds like instruments
playing. The Holy Ghost sings through the
people. God is working in mysterious ways

these days, and I bless Him for it.

The early rain and the much more abundant latter rain were promised in the same month. Now we have the rain of the Spirit with the same power and gifts as in the early church.

> *Lord, how I desire to sing unto You and praise You in the Spirit. Amen.*

9/10/08

Day 28

Greater Works

*Verily, verily, I say unto you, He that
believeth on me, the works that I do shall
he do also; and greater works than these
shall he do; because I go unto my Father.*
—JOHN 14:12

JESUS HAS LEFT His work in our hands. It means something wonderful to be baptized in the Holy Ghost. The Jews were unbelieving until they heard the Holy Ghost speaking in other tongues through those unlearned people. They knew it was God. They realized they had crucified the Lord, that He had risen and gone to glory, and they cried out, "What shall we do?"

Jesus prayed on the cross, "Father, forgive them, for they know not what they do." When the Holy Ghost came they knew what they had done. The "tongues" were a sign to unbelievers. Today it is one of the greatest things God ever did.

The Holy Ghost will sing through us: He is

training us to sing at the marriage supper of the Lamb. We shall not all die, but we shall all be changed. We shall have a glorious body, like Jesus, and shall rise to meet Him in the air, full of joy.

People who are healed are full of joy and sometimes jump and dance when the healing power comes into them. The Holy Ghost takes all the deadness and stiffness out of them; sometimes God slays them and lays them down so He can talk to them.

Men and women, rejoice, seek the baptism, and receive the gifts. You shall have them if you believe for them; and you shall be witnesses. May God seal this in your heart, in the name of Jesus.

> *Jesus, use me to do Your works that God the Father might be glorified. Amen.*

Day 29

Former and Latter Rain

Behold, the husbandman waiteth for the precious fruit of the earth, and hath long patience for it, until he receive the early and latter rain.

—JAMES 5:7

IN THE EAST they had the early rain to start the grain. They could not tell anything about the harvest until they received the latter rain. If it came abundantly there would be a good harvest.

The apostle says to us, "Wait for the latter rain; be ye also patient unto the coming of the Lord." When the latter rain is falling we know the coming of the Lord is near. We are getting the early rain, and will get the latter rain before long. He is getting the bride ready.

The apostle is speaking to the church. If any one is sick among you, don't run for the doctor or send him to the hospital, but let the sick ones send for the elders. The elders were supposed to be men endued with the Holy Ghost, who would come and pray over him, anointing him with oil, and he should be raised up. If he had sinned in any way, he must confess it, and through prayer, be forgiven.

Some people say this is spiritual healing. They are blind because they want to be. Anointing with oil is a symbol of the anointing with the Holy Ghost. A barrel of oil would not heal. But if you are anointing with faith and obedience, you will get the blessing.

It is the healing virtue of Jesus and the power of God. After the disease is cast out, the healing power of Jesus comes in. The prayer of faith shall save the sick. The power of God cleanses the soul, and the sick one is raised up, both soul and body.

> *Rain of God, fall on me, that my dryness might be flooded and Your power might cleanse me soul and body. Amen.*

9/12/08

Pray With the Sick

*And the prayer of faith shall save the sick,
and the Lord shall raise him up; and if he
have committed sins, they shall be forgiven.*
—JAMES 5:15

ANY OF GOD'S CHILDREN, filled with the Holy Ghost, can pray with the sick, anointing with oil in the name of the Lord. You can rely upon it: the person will be raised up.

You can pray for and anoint the sick without any special gift. Pray for one another. People may die before help can reach them. Call in the neighbors, and unite in prayer. If there has been any backbiting confess it.

The prayer of faith is effectual, and availeth much. If you cannot get anyone with a special gift, pray for each other. I know many people who have not had a doctor in the family. Parents pray for the children, and children pray for the parents. Little ones who can hardly talk will pray, and the sick are raised up.

Pray one for another. Wherever you are Jesus is. He is the healer and also the baptizer. He gives the resurrection life. Many today are wonderfully healed while alone with God. God is moving in a marvelous way. We must exercise faith and obedience.

Lord, teach me effectual prayer. Amen.

Day 31

Healing and Salvation

Who forgiveth all thine iniquities; who healeth all thy diseases.

—PSALMS 103:3

SINNERS CANNOT EXPECT to be healed* unless they give their hearts to God. Jesus said, "Thy sins are forgiven," then He healed.

God did not promise to heal sinners, and let then them go forth to serve the devil. He said, "Sin no more, lest a worse thing come unto thee" (John 5:14).

Lord Jesus, I am a sinner. Save me. I am sick. Heal me. Amen.

*NOT true. Sinners can be healed —— by His mercy. Believers are healed by covenant

Day 32

Laying on Hands

They shall lay hands on the sick, and they shall recover.

—MARK 16:18

I WAS HOLDING a meeting in Indiana; there were few people there to pray the power down. Dr. Daggett, a physician, came to the meetings whenever he could and would lead in prayer.

Sometimes he had to go out, he suffered so with pain in his knees. The Lord began to say to me, "That man ought to be healed." He impressed this upon me so much, I had to go to him and say, "I wish you did not have to go out; I need you here."

He said, "I am very sorry, but I suffer so I have to go." I asked him if he did not believe God could heal him, and told him that I believed God wanted to heal him.

God was working with him in the same

way. So I called the congregation together and said, "Are there any Christians here who believe God can heal? If you really believe, come and help me. I am going to pray for healing."

Several came. I did not know what to do any more than a baby. I began to pray; the power of the Lord raised my right arm up until it was over Dr. Daggett's knee and then stopped, for I did not like to touch it. The power of God was in my hand, and He wanted me to lay my hand on that man's knee.

When I understood what God wanted, I laid my hand on the knee and asked God to take the disease out. Dr. Daggett sprang to his feet, healed. He had been in discomfort for twelve years; everyone knew him, and everyone was amazed.

> *Lord, give me the faith to lay hands on the sick, praying for them to be healed. Amen.*

9|15|08

Day 33

Eye Hath Not Seen

Eye hath not seen, nor ear heard, neither hath entered into the heart of man, the things which God hath prepared for them that love him.

—1 CORINTHIANS 2:9

MANY TODAY apply this to eternity or to the other world. They think we never know these things until we get into another world. I am glad the scripture explains itself. "Eye hath not seen," in the natural state. God hath—in the present—revealed the things of God unto us by His Spirit. How? By His Spirit in this world. "The Spirit searcheth all things; yea, the deep things of God."

I call your attention to 1 Corinthians 2:14: "The natural man receiveth not the things of the Spirit of God: for they are foolishness unto him: neither can he know them, because they are spiritually discerned."

The natural man cannot understand this wonderful scripture. There are two classes of men: the spiritual man and the natural man. The natural man is in the "gall of bitterness." The spiritual man is born of God and walks in the Spirit. He gets out into the deep. The natural man can never discern spiritual things, and can never hear and understand the work of the Lord—these things pass all human understanding. The wisdom of this world, intellect and science, can never understand the spiritual things of God.

Holy Spirit, teach me to understand spiritual things. Amen.

Day 34

Wisdom

For it is written, I [God] will destroy the wisdom of the wise, and will bring to nothing the understanding of the prudent.
—1 CORINTHIANS 1:19

THERE ARE two kinds of wisdom: the *wisdom of this world* is foolishness with God; the *wisdom from above* the natural man cannot comprehend. It never enters his imagination to think of the things God hath prepared for those who love Him.

God hath prepared wondrous things already, and He hath revealed them to us by His Spirit. His Spirit lets us down into the deep things, even the deep things of God. This is what we preach, what we practice, and what we stand on. The work of the Spirit is foolishness to the natural man; but he that hath the Spirit can discern spiritual things.

There are many kinds of power, and many spirits going out in the world today. We are told to try the spirits because they are many. Everything is revealed by God through the blessed Holy Ghost. There is only one Spirit with whom we want anything to do with. We want nothing to do with our own spirit, nor any other spirit, but only with the Spirit of the living God. As many as are led by the Spirit of God, they are the sons of God. He will lead us into all truth, all the way; He will lead us where we can get the truth. The child of God will be lead into the baptism of the Holy Ghost and fire and the Pentecostal baptism.

Then we can go from one deep thing to another. The Holy Ghost is sent to us by Jesus Christ, and all gifts come through the Holy Ghost. Jesus said the Holy Ghost would not speak of Himself, but of Jesus. The Holy Spirit will speak to you and show you the things to come. We believe it. Glory to God!

> *Holy Spirit, reveal to me the difference between Your wisdom and the wisdom of this world. Amen.*

Day 35

The Power of God

That your faith should not stand in the wisdom of men, but in the power of God.
—1 CORINTHIANS 2:5

THERE ARE MANY powers in the world, that are not of God, but are counterfeit. But where there is a counterfeit power there is always a genuine power. No one ever tries to counterfeit anything that is not genuine—a sure evidence that it is genuine.

The devil shows his power in a good many ways to deceive people. He tries to substitute some other power for the power of God. It was so in the time of Moses and the time of the prophets. God's power was in the world—especially so at certain times. Then magicians would come up with their powers and show something that seemed similar. One power was God and the other power was the devil.

Moses went to Egypt to lead the people out. He threw down his rod before Pharaoh and it became a living serpent. The magicians said they had the same power, so they threw some rods down, and their rod's became serpents. Moses did not get scared and run away. He knew the power of God and he wouldn't have run if all the serpents in Egypt had come before him.

He stood his ground, and I admire him for it. I do not like a coward. What was the result? Moses' serpent swallowed the others up, head and tail! There was nothing left of them. Those who are trying to overthrow the power of God and substitute something else will have a day of judgment. The time is coming when the Almighty power of God will swallow them up, the day of His wrath.

Lord, I pray that my faith does not rely on the wisdom of men but upon Your power. Amen.

Teach me to get out of Your way & stay there so You can work.

Day 36

The Power of the Holy Ghost

Now the God of hope fill you with all joy and peace in believing, that ye may abound in hope, through the power of the Holy Ghost.

—ROMANS 15:13

THE LAMB OF GOD left the realms of glory, and came down here to be footsore, dusty, weary, and scorned. He said, "I am come to do Thy will, Oh God." If He had not borne all these things and had not gone all the way to the cross, the Holy Ghost never could have come. If He had been left in the tomb, the Holy Ghost never could have come. As soon as He arose from the dead and ascended into Heaven, the Holy Ghost could come.

God gave His Son the highest place before all the hosts of Heaven; then He sent the Holy Ghost to dwell in these bodies, His temple. The Holy Ghost is a great power. He is compared to wind, water, and fire.

At Pentecost He came like a cyclone and a

mighty rushing wind. He is to come like rivers
of living water. He comes as fire. Tongues of
fire sat upon each of the hundred and twenty
people at Pentecost. Wind, water, and fire—
the most destructive elements we have, yet the
most useful.

God uses them to denote the mighty power
of the Holy Ghost; and He was to be given
after Jesus was glorified. We see many demonstrations of His mighty power, and we can but
"speak the things we have seen and heard," of
His glory and majesty. When we know these
things, we are witnesses to His power, majesty,
and glory. Glory to God!

> *Holy Spirit, come over me like wind,
> water, and fire. Baptize me in Your
> power. Amen.*

Day 37

Experiencing God's Power

For the preaching of the cross is to them that perish foolishness; but unto us which are saved it is the power of God.
—1 CORINTHIANS 1:18

IN THE BIBLE we read how men fell when they caught a glimpse of God's glory. Paul tells us there are those who have a form of godliness, but deny the power thereof; from such we are to turn away. "In the last days, perilous times shall come," and those who have reprobate minds shall withstand God's children to their faces, even as the magicians withstood Moses.

In the last days, there will be some people living very near to God; but the devil will have his workers, too, who will attribute signs and wonders done to any power except the power of Christ. The Lamb of God, the Lion of the tribe of Judah, has never lost His power, and never will lose His power. I would hate to say, by my actions, that I thought the devil had more power than God.

There is a wonderful difference between the power of God and any of those other powers. The Holy Ghost comes only in Christ. He only comes into the bodies of those who love God. When He takes possession of us, He takes us away into the sweetest experience this side of heaven—that of being alone with God. He talks to us and reveals to us "things to come" (John 16).

It is wonderful! God puts us under the power, and God takes us out. No man can bestow this power upon another. It comes only through Jesus Christ. There are two kinds of power, and people who do not know the difference will stand up today and say that wisdom is foolishness.

> *Holy Spirit, take possession of me that*
> *I might know the sweetest experience*
> *this side of heaven. Amen.* Amen

Day 38

Signs of the Holy Ghost

*And these signs shall follow them that
believe.*

—MARK 16:17

MANY PEOPLE today have an intellectual
faith and a historical faith. They believe.
Well, the devils believe and tremble. Belief is
one thing, but faith is another. "The letter kil-
leth; the Spirit giveth life." If the truth is hid,
it is hid to those who are lost.

We may have intellectual imaginations, go
through a course of study, and learn the doctrines of men. However, no one but the Holy
Ghost can even give us knowledge of "the
things of God." They seem foolishness to the
natural man. Sometimes the Holy Ghost gives
a spirit of laughter, and sometimes one of
weeping, with everyone in the place being
affected by the Spirit.

I have stood before thousands of people,

and could not speak, just weep. When I was able to see, people were weeping everywhere. That is one way the Holy Ghost works. I have stood for an hour with my hand raised, held by the mighty power of God. When I came to myself and saw the people, their faces were shining.

God moves in mysterious ways His wonders to perform. He is the God I worship. Jesus says, "Behold I and the children which God hath given me" (Heb. 2:13). We believe in signs and wonders, not from beneath but from above. We are a people to be wondered at. We are a sign among the people.

> *Lord, through Your power make of me a sign to others, pointing to You. Amen.*

Day 39

Noah's Ark and Our Faith

*By faith Noah, being warned of God of
things not seen as yet, moved with fear,
prepared an ark to the saving of his house.*
—HEBREWS 11:7

MANY THINGS recorded in the Old
Testament are types of the work of the
Spirit in the New Testament. Many of the
movements of God through His children
seemed foolish, and the messages God gave
His prophets to carry, humanly speaking,
seemed very foolish.

He gave Noah a plan of the ark—with only
one window and one door. He built it
according to God's plan, not heeding the jeers
of the people who thought he was losing his
mind. He was a gazing stock for everybody,
but he went on with the building, and proved
the wisdom of God in the end.

He built the ark, and God provided the
water. There was more water than they

wanted, too much water for them. What happened? God took those who believed Him into the ark and shut the door. The water rose, and the ark went above the treetops—as we are going some day. God is building the ark now; and the works of the Holy Ghost are foolishness to the people who are fighting them.

The ark sailed away, and the world went down, all except Noah and his family. Not many are going into the ark God is building. People are crying, "Foolishness."

Jesus, You are my ark of salvation. The foolishness of Your cross is the wisdom of salvation for my life. Amen.

Day 40

Joshua, Jericho, and Faith

*By faith the walls of Jericho fell down,
after they were compassed about seven
days.*

—HEBREWS 11:30

TRULY, God moves in a mysterious way. Remember the fall of Jericho. It had great walls around it, and all the people were shut in. God said to Joshua that he and his men of war should march around the city once a day for six days, with seven priests bearing before the ark seven trumpets of rams' horns. On the seventh day they were to march around the city seven times, with the priests blowing with the trumpets. When they made a long trumpet blast the people were to shout, and the walls should fall down.

It took faith to do all that marching without any sign of victory; to shout—anyone can shout after the walls fall. Humanly speaking, how foolish this all was, don't you see? No preparation for war, only marching and blowing rams' horns, but that was God's way, and they were silly enough to obey God! What was the result? The walls went down.

So we could go through all the Word of God. So many things that seem so silly. God asked His people to do things people would laugh at, but it was God's way, and His servants were willing to obey Him. The result showed God's wonderful wisdom and brought victory through a visible display of His power.

> *Lord, give me the courage to do whatever You ask no matter how foolish it may seem to the world so that Your power may be manifested in my life. Amen.*

9/23/08

Day 41

The Deep Things of God

But God hath revealed them unto us by his Spirit: for the Spirit searcheth all things, yea, the deep things of God.
—1 CORINTHIANS 2:10

THE SPIRIT OF GOD lets us down into the deep things, even the deep things of God. Peter fell into a trance upon the house-top, and God spoke to him three times. Paul and Silas started out to visit converts. Paul had a vision; he saw a man of Macedonia holding out his hands and saying, "Come over and help us." He knew it was the call of God, so they changed their course and went to a place altogether different than their plans.

When Paul and Silas began to preach and were arrested, they might have thought they had been mistaken about God's call. But Paul knew God, and he never doubted it was God's voice that had called him. They might have said, "We would have had many people to preach to if we had not come here, but now we have been put in prison with our feet fast in the stocks." The devil put them in there, but God permitted it, and God delivered them.

There are many wonderful things for us in these last days—demonstrations of God's power which the natural man cannot understand. There are other powers too, and many do not know the difference. God's power is the greatest, and is the only power that will bring peace to your soul.

God, reveal to me the deep things of Your Spirit that I may know You. Amen.

Day 42

The Sacrifice of Praise

*By him, therefore let us offer the sacrifice
of praise to God continually, that is, the
fruit of our lips giving thanks to his name.*
—HEBREWS 13:15

"LET EVERYTHING that hath breath praise
the Lord." People ask why we tell them
to praise the Lord.

If you do not feel it at first, then offer your
praise as a "sacrifice." Praise is not a feeling but
an act of obedient sacrifice. After the sacrifice
of praise, comes the praise itself, out of a soul
filled with joy. The result of praise is joy
unspeakable!

Hallelujah!

*Lord, to You I bring my sacrifice of
praise. Amen.*

4/25/08

Day 43

Glory Fills the Temple

The house was filled with a cloud . . . So that the priests could not stand to minister by reason of the cloud: for the glory of the Lord had filled the house of God.
—2 CHRONICLES 5:13–14

I WANT YOU to see how they came. One hundred twenty of them with different instruments, yet all making the same sound. The Levites were arrayed in white linen, emblematic of purity. "It came even to pass, as the trumpeters and singers were as one, to make one sound to be heard in praising and thanking the Lord; and when they lifted up their voice with the trumpets and cymbals and instruments of music, and praised the Lord . . . " (2 Chron. 5:13).

Then the house was filled with a cloud, even the house of the Lord. The priests could not stand to minister by reason of the cloud; for the glory of the Lord had filled the "house of God." The priests could not stand, and the entire place was filled with the glory of God.

All this demonstration of the glory of God was brought about by the one hundred twenty priests who blew the trumpets and instruments that mingled with the voice of the great company of singers. The whole object was to glorify God with one sound.

God wants perfect harmony. No one criticizing, no one finding fault, but all sounding forth His praise in purity. If we go out to meet God clothed in white, washed in the blood of the Lamb; if we all go out making the same sound; if we go out to glorify God; God will honor all the noise.

> *Lord, how I want Your glory to fill this temple of my body so that Your glory may be revealed to those around me. Amen.*

9/26/08

Day 44

God's Glory

*Now when Solomon had made an end of
praying, the fire came down from heaven,
and consumed the burnt offering . . . and
the glory of the Lord filled the house.*

—2 CHRONICLES 7:1

IT REPRESENTED PENTECOST: "When Solomon
had made an end of praying." So many
people expect God to answer. They would be
frightened if He did. Solomon stretched out
his hands and prayed to God, and God heard
him.

When he had made an end of praying,
something happened. God will come forth if
you are not afraid of the power, if you are
ready to stand for God with all there is of you.
As Pentecostal people we should always be
"prayed up," so we can get hold of God
quickly, and be sure it is for the glory of God.

"The fire came down from heaven, and
consumed the burnt offering and the sacri-
fices; and the glory of the Lord filled the

house" (v. 1). Some people talk as if God never had any glory, as though the glory of God was never seen at any time.

Paul said, "For if the ministration of condemnation be glory, much more doth the ministration of righteousness exceed in glory" (2 Cor. 3:9).

The glory under the law did not last; but the Holy Ghost came at Pentecost to stay. And the manifestations under the ministry of the Holy Ghost are to be with much greater glory, to "exceed in glory." The power under the law was only a shadow of what we ought to have under grace. This was the ministry of life, not death.

Lord, minister Your glory to me. Amen.

Day 45

𝕶𝖊𝖊𝖕 𝖙𝖍𝖊 𝕷𝖆𝖒𝖕 𝕭𝖚𝖗𝖓𝖎𝖓𝖌

*What? know ye not that your body is the
temple of the Holy Ghost which is in you,
which ye have of God, and ye are not your
own?*

—1 CORINTHIANS 6:19

IF THE GLORY of God came down and the
people fell prostrate in Solomon's day,
how much glory ought there to be today?
There was just one tabernacle and two tables
of stone. Today your body is the temple of the
living God. Our bodies are the temple of the
Holy Ghost—and God with His own finger
writes His Word in our hearts.

The ancient temple in all its glory repre-
sents each one of our bodies. If we are filled
with the Holy Ghost as we ought to be, the body
will be flooded with rivers of water, flowing
out to others, and it will be on fire for God.

The glory of the Lord was seen over the ark;
inside the tabernacle the lamp was always
burning, being kept supplied with oil. It never

went out. In the temple of the body, God puts His love in our hearts, and He wants us to keep the light always burning; never letting the fire of the Holy Spirit go out.

> *Continually burn within me, O Fire of God. Amen.*

Day 46

One in the Spirit

*That they all may be one; as thou, Father,
art in me, and I in thee, that they also
may be one in us: that the world may
believe that thou hast sent me.*

—JOHN 17:21

BY KEEPING all obstructions out of the channel of faith, we get a continual supply of oil; and the light shall shine through the tabernacle always. If the oracle written on stone was glorious, how much more glorious under grace! The Holy Ghost shall abide with you always.

Jesus said that if we keep His commandments, the Father and He would both take up their abode with us. They dwell with us, and we are flooded with the Holy Ghost. We become people to be wondered at. We are one with Him and with one another in the Spirit.

At the dedication of Solomon's temple, "all the congregation of Israel stood" as the glory of the Lord filled the house of God. (2 Chron.

6:3). The glory came down at Solomon's prayer of dedication. At a glimpse of that glory the congregation lost their strength and the whole multitude "bowed their faces to the ground . . . and worshiped, and praised the Lord" (2 Chron. 7:3). There should be perfect fellowship and harmony, we are to be one in the Spirit.

> *Father, make us one in Your Spirit*
> *that we may perfectly give You glory.*
> *Amen.*

9/29/08

Day 47

God's Power Shines Forth

*Go and shew John again those things
which ye do hear and see . . .*
—MATTHEW 11:4

WHAT A WONDERFUL people we are in our privileges! Today everyone may be God's priest. If we abide in Him and His words abide in us, we may ask what we will and it shall be done. We indeed have wonderful privileges. The power of the Lord shines forth a hundred times greater than under the law.

When John was in prison he began to doubt whether Jesus was the Christ, and he sent his disciples to ask, "Art Thou He that should come?" Jesus did not say, "I belong to the church or I belong to a college." He told John's disciples to tell John the things they have seen: the lame walked, the blind could see, different diseases were healed, and the poor had the gospel preached to them. "Blessed is he, whosoever shall not be offended" (Matt. 11:6). Men get mad at the signs of the Holy Ghost. They become jealous, spitting out hatred and trying to tear down God's work.

If John did not believe in Christ through the signs, no eloquence would be of value. If he did not believe what the witnesses told him he would not believe anything.

Neither will you! If you only look on, it will seem foolishness to you as we praise God, get filled with the Holy Ghost and get gifts. But it is Jesus first, last, and all the time. We hold up Jesus and praise His name. We see bright, happy faces. We see pain go out of bodies, and we go home rejoicing.

> *Lord Jesus, help me to move beyond the traditions of men and into Your power, signs, and wonders. Amen.*

9/30/08

The Joy of Unity

Fulfill ye my joy, that ye be like-minded, having the same love, being of one accord, of one mind.

—PHILIPPIANS 2:2

ARE YOU FULL of joy, having not a doubt about Jesus being your Lord and Savior? You want power to do the work of God. You want to be clothed with power. God says He will baptize with fire, bestowing wisdom, knowledge, and gifts. He will make you understand the deep things of God, and as you teach them and live them, God will be with you.

You must believe you are going to get this blessing. The people were "with one accord." God help us to get to that place. God wants us of one accord with our hearts running together like drops of water.

A little company of one mind like the early church could shake a city in a day. We are not in one accord when one is pulling one way, and one another—when we hear "maybe this," and "maybe that." Do you suppose God will bless you in that?

You cannot understand the first principles. Once you have the newborn joy in your heart, when you see it in someone else, you know it is of God. Be of one mind; no matter how much you have to praise God for, we always want more.

Father, give our church unity in joy. Amen.

10/1/08

Day 49

Suddenly

*And suddenly there came a sound from
heaven as of a rushing mighty wind, and
it filled all the house.*

—ACTS 2:2

AT PENTECOST, suddenly they heard a
sound like a mighty, rushing wind. This
Holy Ghost we are holding up is a mighty
power. He came *suddenly* from heaven, like a
windstorm, like floods of water filling the vessels, and as fire upon the heads of one hundred
twenty people.

As it were, cloven tongues of fire sat upon
their heads. Then the Holy Ghost went in and
took possession of the temple. He took full
possession of the machinery, wound it up and
set it running for God. They staggered like
drunken people and fell. This mighty power
took possession of their tongues, and spoke
through them in other languages.

It said away back in the times of the

prophets God said that through men of "stammering lips and another tongue will He speak to this people." Think of that! God's doing such a mighty thing! But some do not want to believe. That is the way the Holy Ghost came, and still comes today; and people say it is some other power.

They did not lose their minds; they had just found them! They had the spirit of love and of a sound mind. We never have a sound mind until we get the mind of Christ. People who cannot understand, say these things are foolishness. We are told the wisdom of this world is foolishness with God. This is the power and wisdom of God, not the work of the devil; people saying so doesn't make it so.

God had complete control. *Suddenly,* He came in and took possession. The Holy Ghost is in the world today.

> *Suddenly come over me, Holy Spirit,*
> *and transform me with Your fire.*
> *Amen.*

Day 50

The Ministry of the Holy Spirit

But the manifestation of the Spirit is given to every man to profit.
—1 CORINTHIANS 12:7

THE PROFESSIONAL ministry does not want the gifts today. Christians are baptized with the Holy Ghost that the whole body may be edified.

The working of the Holy Ghost is the visible sign of the presence of Jesus. They went from Jerusalem to preach the gospel, and the Lord was with them. I love that word. He is in heaven—but He is also with us.

The Lord was with them, confirming the Word. How? With signs and wonders following. Wherever they went they saw faces shine, someone healed, someone speaking in tongues. This you see and hear—it is the Holy Ghost—and it is for the work of the ministry. We do not need professional ministers.

Everyone filled with the Holy Ghost can minister in the gifts.

I have tested the truth; I know it is of God. How can we help talking of the things we have seen? I have seen things by the Spirit, and in visions. I have seen Jesus; the heavens open; the marriage supper; hosts of angels; the glory of God. I have seen them, glory to God! I know what I am telling you. I know Jesus lives and is standing by my side more truly than I know you are here. These things are verities.

I am not ashamed of the Gospel of Christ. Glory to God! When a weak woman comes here to tell you what strong men in the ministry ought to have told you, what are you going to think about it? I say these things are true; and when people say they are foolishness and fanaticism, dare they attempt to prove it by the Word? I dare them to do it.

> *God, give me boldness to minister with the Spirit's gifts, no matter what. Amen.*

Day 51

Dancing in the Spirit

Let them praise his name in the dance: let them sing praises unto him with the timbrel and harp.

—PSALMS 149:3

IN THESE LAST DAYS, when God is pouring out His Spirit in great cloudbursts and tidal waves from the floodgates of heaven, and the great river of life is flooding our spirit and body and baptizing us with fire and resurrection life, the Lord is doing His acts. Some of His acts may appear strange, like dancing in the Spirit, speaking in other tongues, and many other operations and gifts. The Holy Ghost is confirming the last message of the coming King, with great signs, wonders, and miracles.

If you read carefully what the Scripture says about dancing, you will be surprised, and will see that singing, music, and dancing has a humble and holy place in the Lord's church.

"Praise Him with the timbrel and dance" (Ps. 150:4). So praise Him with the timbrel and the dance, praise Him with the stringed instruments and organ. Jeremiah 31:15 says, "Then shall the virgin rejoice in the dance, both young men and old together."

I dance before You with joy, O my King Jesus. Amen.

Day 52

Praise and Dancing

And Miriam the prophetess . . . took a timbrel in her hand; and all the women went out after her with timbrels and dances.

—EXODUS 15:20

GOD HAS never done a greater miracle or demonstrated His presence in so great a cloud of glory as at the time of Miriam. While under the inspiration and light of His presence, their whole bodies and spirits going out in love, the whole multitude of women led by Miriam the prophetess, praised the Lord with dancing, shouting, and music, singing a new song that had never been sung just given to them by the Spirit.

Do you call that foolishness? No, they were praising the Lord in the dance and song as they were moved in and by the power of God.

Moses also led the hosts in the same way, with music and dancing, and a new song given for the occasion by the Spirit. So the Holy

Ghost is falling on the saints of God today, and they are used the same way. Those who never danced one step are experts in the holy dance, and those who do not know one note from another are expert musicians, in playing many different instruments of music. Often the sounds of invisible instruments also can be plainly heard all over the house.

And I say, in the fear and presence of God, the singing and demonstration puts the fear of God on the people and causes a holy hush to come over the people. The strange acts are coming more and more, showing they are something new, and that Jesus is coming soon. The Lord is getting His bride ready to be translated, to dance and play at the great marriage of the Lamb.

> *With joy, I dance before You, My Lord Jesus, declaring Your praises, for You have won every victory. Amen.*

Day 53

Rejoice in the Dance

Then shall the virgin rejoice in the dance,
both young men and old together: for I
will turn their mourning into joy.
—JEREMIAH 31:13

I WAS VERY SLOW to accept dancing in the
Spirit for fear it was in the flesh, but I
soon saw it was the "cloud of glory" over the
people that brought forth the dancing, and
playing of invisible instruments. The sounds
of sweet, heavenly music could often be heard.
Several times I asked that those of the congregation who heard this music from the
platform (where they knew there were no
instruments to be seen), to be honest and raise
their hands. The stillness of death went over
the people when they heard the sounds of
music, accompanied with the heavenly choir.

Often a message in tongues was given in
one or more languages, and the interpretation.
As I saw the effect that the Holy Ghost had on

the people, convincing them that they were in the presence of God, I concluded that this is surely the Lord's strange work and His strange acts. I saw as many as nine of the most noted ministers dancing at one time on the platform; they danced single, with their eyes closed; often some fell, slain by the mighty power of God. These things convinced me. One lady who was on crutches for five years, got healed in her seat and afterward danced around the platform, singing heavenly music.

The virgins, the young men, and the old men, all join in the dance together. Praise the Lord. "Let us be glad and rejoice, and give honor to him: for the marriage of the Lamb is come, and his wife hath made herself ready" (Rev. 19:7).

> *Let Your cloud of glory descend upon me, causing my feet to dance in Your presence and my ears to hear the choirs of heaven. Amen.*

10/6/08

Day 54

The Spirit's Outpouring

And it shall come to pass in the last days,
saith God, I will pour out of my Spirit
upon all flesh . . . And I will show wonders
in heaven above. . . .

—ACTS 2:17, 19

THIS IS A wonderful scripture, and many do not understand it. There is a certain time spoken of here, when certain great and wonderful things shall take place and people shall know that prophecy is being fulfilled. "It shall come to pass in the last days, I will pour out My Spirit," and there shall be signs in the heavens and the earth—signs of His coming.

This prophecy was first spoken eight hundred years before Jesus came to earth. Peter, standing up on the day of Pentecost, confirmed it. Under the inspiration of the Holy Ghost, on fire with the Holy Ghost from head to foot, he said these things would come to pass in the last days.

We believe and know by the Word of God,

and by the signs, that we are now living in the last days; the very times Peter spoke about when we were to know by the mighty things taking place. We are the people, and this is the time just before the "notable day of the Lord" bursts upon the world. We believe we are the people, yea we know it.

> *Almighty God, how I rejoice in the outpouring of Your Holy Spirit. Amen.*

Day 55

Ready for the Flood

I will pour out of my Spirit upon all flesh.
—ACTS 2:17

NOT SPRINKLE a few drops, but pour out on all flesh—a cloudburst! Just at the end; it will continue until the saints are taken away; then the tribulation will burst upon the earth. The sign will be that your sons and daughters, not everybody's—*your sons and daughters*—shall prophesy. It is very plain so that everyone may understand.

"Your sons and your daughters will prophesy." There is to be a wonderful ministry in the last days. Paul says male and female are one in Christ. Both shall prophesy in the last days.

That is the effect of the outpouring of the Holy Ghost. And there are other signs:

- devils shall be cast out

- hands shall be laid on the sick, and they shall recover
- if anyone drinks poison accidentally, it shall not hurt him; many shall speak with new tongues
- serpents shall not be able to hurt believers in the last days

Are you under the cloudburst? Are you ready for the Spirit's flood?

> *Lord, I am ready. Flood me with Your Spirit. Amen.*

Day 56

Jesus' Bride

That he might present it to himself a glorious church, not having spot, or wrinkle, or any such thing; but that it should be holy and without blemish.

—EPHESIANS 5:27

GOD IS PREPARING His spiritual ark today. The body of Christ will soon be complete, and when it is complete it will go above the treetops to meet our Lord and King in the air. We are in the day of preparation of the King of glory, and His bride is making herself ready. Rejoice and be glad, for the marriage of the Lamb is at hand. The bride must be arrayed in white linen and the robe of righteousness, clothed in the power of the Holy Spirit.

She is getting her garments ready to meet the Bridegroom. I praise the Lord that I am living in this day. The bride will be caught up just before the tribulation bursts upon this sin-cursed earth. The bride must be very beautiful. She is represented as a queen dressed in a robe of finest needlework. She will shine with the gifts and jewels of the Holy Ghost.

We have this treasure in earthen vessels. But they that be wise shall shine as the brightness of the sun, and the wise shall know when these things are coming, when the ark is about ready to go up. The Lord will not keep any secrets from them, as there is perfect confidence between the bride and the Bridegroom. So Jesus will reveal secrets to His bride.

A bride is very happy. She is willing to forsake her father's house, her friends, everything, and go with her Bridegroom, even to a foreign country. She loves those she leaves, but He is dearer to her than anything else.

The bride will be taken out, and men and women will be left. You may say, "I do not believe it." *I believe it!*

Lord Jesus, prepare Your bride, the church, for the wedding feast. Amen.

Day 57

𝔚𝔬𝔯𝔡𝔰 𝔗𝔥𝔞𝔱 𝔖𝔥𝔞𝔨𝔢 𝔱𝔥𝔢 𝔚𝔬𝔯𝔩𝔡

And my speech and my preaching was not with enticing words of man's wisdom, but in demonstration of the Spirit and of power.

—1 CORINTHIANS 2:4

PAUL SAID his teaching was not with enticing words of man's wisdom, but in demonstration of the Spirit and of power. That shakes the world, and it is just the same today. You say you do not like this power. Well, the devil does not like it either. I have been out in the work for thirty-five years, and people fell under the power by thousands before I preached healing.

There were mighty outpourings of the Spirit that made the devil howl. It shows how little we know of the real gospel when we take the letter of the law. It is like skimmed milk. No man can understand the deep things of God except by the Spirit.

Paul had much knowledge, but He said the

wisdom of this world was foolishness in the sight of God. True wisdom comes from heaven. The Word must be preached in simplicity. Jesus had the eloquence of high heaven at His command, yet He used language that the most uneducated could understand.

Jesus, give me words to declare with simplicity Your gospel. Amen.

10/10/08

Day 58

To See God's Throne

And they chose Stephen, a man full of faith and of the Holy Ghost.

—ACTS 6:5

REMEMBER THE first martyr, Stephen? He was a man full of faith, wisdom, and power. He was full of the Holy Ghost. The wise men tried to confound him, but could not do it; then they were jealous and wanted to get rid of him. They hired men of the baser sort, who lied about this mighty servant of God.

They arrested him, and there he was before the great assembly. He did not try to defend himself, but he took the opportunity offered to preach to them about Jesus. He was filled with the Holy Ghost. His face was as the face of an angel, and those who swore his life away saw it. He did not look like a liar and a hypocrite. He was a servant of Almighty God.

Sometimes you can see that light today in the faces of God's children. Stephen looked up into heaven and saw the glory of God. He saw Jesus who had risen from the dead, standing at the right hand of God, and he told the people, "Oh, Lord, open the eyes of these people, and let them see the angels of the Lord encamped around about us and Jesus standing in the midst!" When Stephen told what he saw, the evil men gnashed their teeth. They did not intend to repent. They dragged him out and stoned him to death, but the Lord received him and permitted it. God promises His people shall be protected, and it is no sign that He forsakes them because trouble comes. Stephen's enemies did not like it because God received him, nor did they like to see his face shine with the glory of God. His body was lying a bruised mass, but he rose to meet the Lord. He had a glorious vision.

Lord Jesus, I long to see the Father's throne and You standing there as Stephen did. Amen.

10/11/08

Not I, But Christ

*Then Peter said, Silver and gold have I
none, but, such as I have give I thee: In
the name of Jesus Christ of Nazareth rise
up and walk.*

—ACTS 3:6

IN THE New Testament, signs and wonders
were done before the people. Wherever
Jesus went, the people followed Him. God was
with Him, putting fear upon the people
through miracles, signs, and wonders that
God wrought through Him.

He said, "I speak not of myself: but the
Father that dwelleth in me, he doeth the
works" (John 14:10). When the rulers, elders,
and scribes demanded to know from Peter:
"By what power, or by what name, have ye
done this [healed the impotent man]?", Peter
responded: "Be it known unto you all, and to
all the people of Israel, that by the name of
Jesus Christ of Nazareth, whom ye crucified,
whom God raised from the dead even by him

doth this man stand here before you whole"
(Acts 4:7, 10). Not I, but Christ. It is the same
today.

In the signs and wonders today, it is "Not I,
but Christ." He dwells in these bodies, and the
work is done by the mighty power of the Holy
Ghost. "Know ye not that your body is the
temple of the Holy Ghost?" Jesus Christ
dwells in us. We are God's powerhouse.

Jesus, I desire to be Your powerhouse.
Amen.

10/12/08

Day 60

Press the Battle to the Gates

*Nay, in all these things we are more than
conquerors through him that loved us.*
—ROMANS 8:37

IT WAS BY the hands of the apostles, not of
angels, that God did His mighty works;
and people believed when the signs followed.
Jesus commanded the unclean spirits to come
out, and they had to come; the power of the
Holy Spirit went through the apostles' hands,
and that is just the way God works today.

The apostles were not afraid of persecution,
the sword, or anything else. They were willing
to face death in any form, rather than disgrace
the cause of Christ by being cowards. It is a
mighty God we serve, and today, Jesus Christ
who ascended into heaven is here by my side.
He will lead His hosts on to victory. Let us
press the battle to the gates.

This sect [Pentecostals] is always spoken
against, misrepresented, and lied about; but

Jesus Christ is leading on His hosts. God permitted Jesus to be nailed to the cross and laid in the grave, but He came forth like the sun.

God permitted the apostles to be arrested, and put in prison; then He had an opportunity to show His power. He sent His angel and delivered them. The angel of the Lord is with His own. Our citizenship is in heaven. We are children of the King.

Around us day and night are ministering spirits sent to minister to those who are heirs of salvation. We can afford to be misrepresented, or even put in prison, if only we are looking for the manifestation and the glory of translation that will sweep us through the gates.

Jesus, I am willing to suffer anything for You. Amen.

Day 61

The Unforgivable Sin

*Wherefore I say unto you, All manner of
sin and blasphemy shall be forgiven unto
men: but the blasphemy against the Holy
Ghost shall not be forgiven unto men.*
—MATTHEW 12:31

THIS MESSAGE comes to us from Jesus
tonight as much as if He were standing
here. Hear the eternal word from the lips of
the Son of God now reigning in glory. The
words are just as powerful as from His lips if
they go out by the power of the Holy Ghost.
This subject is considered one of the deepest
in the Word of God. You have often heard the
question asked, "What is the unpardonable
sin?" And some people are very much con-
cerned about having committed it. John says:
"There is a sin unto death: I do not say that he
shall pray for it" (1 John 5:16).

Blasphemy against God, and all kinds of sin
against Him and against mankind, will be
blotted out, but whosoever speaks against the

Holy Ghost hath no forgiveness, either in this world or in the world to come. Christ said this because the people said that He had an evil spirit and did His mighty works through that evil agency.

So you see, it is an unpardonable sin to attribute any of the mighty works of the Holy Ghost to the devil. There has never been a time since the early church when there was so much danger of people committing the unpardonable sin as there is today. The Pentecostal fire has girdled the earth, and tens of thousands have received the Holy Ghost having felt His presence, backed up by signs, wonders, and diverse operations of the Spirit.

> *Jesus, I love and cherish Your Holy Spirit. Amen.*

10/14/08

Do Not Stifle God's Spirit

Quench not the Spirit.
—1 THESSALONIANS 5:19

E WILL NOT only come in healing power, but will manifest Himself in many mighty ways. On the day of Pentecost, Peter said, "God hath poured forth this which ye see and hear." And from what they heard and saw, three thousand knew it was the power of God and turned to Christ. Others stifled conviction, and turned away saying, "This is the work of the devil."

When the Holy Ghost is poured out, it is either life unto life or death unto death. It is life unto life to those who go forward, and death unto death to those who blaspheme against the Holy Ghost. So we want to be careful what we say against the divers operations, supernatural signs, and workings of the

Holy Ghost. Some people look on and say, "It looks like hypnotism," or "I believe it is mesmerism."

To others it appears mere foolishness, even as Scripture says of the natural man, "The natural man receiveth not the things of the Spirit of God for they are foolishness unto him: neither can he know them, because they are spiritually discerned" (1 Cor. 2:14). Have you received of the life of the Spirit, or are you stifling His conviction?

> *Almighty God, we receive life from You, and never want to quench Your Spirit. Amen.*

Day 63

The Cyclone of the Spirit

Then the Lord answered Job out of the whirlwind.

—JOB 38:1

WE COULD NOT live without fire, wind, or water. When a cyclone comes, men and women turn pale. When God's cyclone through the Holy Ghost strikes the people, it is a great leveler. They lose sight of their money bags. All hatred and ill-will are swept away as a cyclone carries all before it. When a tidal wave strikes a city, it submerges everything. So, in a tidal wave of the Holy Ghost, everything goes under. Oh, we want a cyclone of God's power to sweep out of our lives everything that cumbers us, and a tidal wave to submerge us in God.

God uses these great elements—fire, wind and water—in all their force to give us an idea of the mighty power of the Holy Ghost. Our bodies are His temples and, as great pieces of mechanism are moved by electricity, so our bodies, the most wonderful piece of mechanism ever known, are moved by the power of the Holy Ghost sent down from heaven. He filled the one and twenty on the day of Pentecost with power to witness for Jesus. At the hands of the apostles, God healed the sick, and He heals today by the same power that was on the apostles. God pours out rivers of living waters. What manner of people ought we to be? People living in the cyclone of God's Spirit!

> *Wind of God, blow in and through my life, moving me in only those directions You would have me go. Amen.*

Day 64

The Best Is Yet to Come

Who then is a faithful and wise servant,
whom his lord hath made ruler over his
household, to give them meat in due season?
—MATTHEW 24:45

GOD IS GETTING His children ready to sing at the marriage supper of the Lamb. They sing a song no one can sing except the redeemed. The Spirit has shown me that the coming of the Lord is very near, and I know it now more than ever. God baptized me over twenty-five years ago with a wonderful baptism, but I am more hungry today than I ever was. Let us go on from one degree to another. Blessed is the servant who, when his master comes, is found at his post, giving to the household their portion of meat in due season. This is your opportunity, your day of God's visitation. "The bride hath made herself ready." You cannot go to the tailor and order your suit to go to the banquet. You have to make it yourself. The bride hath made herself ready and it is going to be the most wonderful wedding garment you ever heard of.

It takes skill to weave the garment of pure linen and to embroider the "fine wrought linen work." When she is ready, He will greatly admire her. There will be a great company of guests in the banquet hall. But some of us are not ready. We haven't made our garments. The time has come to get ready. Oh, it means something to dress for the marriage supper of the Lamb. When there is a banquet in honor of the king's son or daughter, it is a great occasion and the musicians are trained for it long before. Now this banquet that is going to take place in the skies, this marriage supper of the Lamb, will be the greatest wedding that was ever known.

> *Lord, I am alert, waiting, and prepared for Your coming. I long to sit at Your banquet table at the wedding feast You have prepared. Amen.*

Day 65

At His Table

Thou preparest a table before me in the presence of mine enemies.

—PSALMS 23:5

THE INTEREST in this meeting has increased in power and number from the first to the last. Jesus says, "If I be lifted up, I will draw all men unto me" (John 12:32). The Master of Assemblies has honored the feast with His glorious presence and continually supplied the table with the bounties of heaven.

Oh, praise the Lord, He prepares the table in the presence of our enemies, and they cannot taste of the feast. Oh! See the beautiful whiteness, the shining brightness of the great loaves of "Living Bread" dropped down from heaven, not like the manna in the wilderness after which people died, but whoso eateth of this bread shall live forever.

Oh, see the table is filled with "a feast of

wine on the lees, fat things full of marrow, of wines on the lees well refined" (Isa. 25:6). See the strong meat to make us mighty in the Lord, and the oil to make us shine so that the beauty of the Lord may be seen in us.

We gather at His table to eat meat, break bread, and drink wine. It is the meat of His Word. It is the bread of His broken body on the cross. It is the wine of His blood shed for our sin. Together, it is the new wine of His Spirit, who fills and baptizes us with power. What a wonderful feast this is!

> *Jesus, how thankful I am to sit at Your table and lift up praise to You for the meat, bread, and wine. Amen.*

10/18/08

Day 66

Forsaking Earthly Things

Jesus said unto him, If thou wilt be per-
fect, go and sell that thou hast, and give
to the poor, and thou shalt have treasure
in heaven: and come and follow me.
—MATTHEW 19:21

OH! BELOVED READERS, the evil days are on us. The awful storm and darkness of the tribulation is now sweeping over us with such force. Unless we get deep, yes, deeper in God, we will not be able to stand against all the powers of hell.

Let us go forward and not tarry. Be willing to forsake every earthly thing, leave our father's house, and worship Him only. He will reveal Himself to us as never before.

Jesus, I surrender all to follow You.
Amen.

Day 67

On Needing a Sign

*And when the people were gathered thick
together, he began to say, This is an evil
generation: they seek a sign; and there
shall no sign be given it.*

—LUKE 11:29

JESUS IS coming soon and we are con-
cerned about the signs. The Lord told
them how they should know. He gave them
signs, and said that when you see certain
things come to pass, prepare to flee to the
mountains and make ready to escape. And
then other signs, and finally a certain sign—
when you see this sign, if you have not made
all preparations for flight, if you are on the
house top and have left anything in the house,
don't take it, but flee to the mountains,
because the gates will be closed and you will be
shut in. They believed what God said. They
took His word by faith. They believed the
word and felt the responsibility.

They loved their people and they knew that

unless they accepted Jesus Christ they would not escape. They were sighing and crying for their own people and their neighbors according to the flesh, and crying on account of the evil things coming, yet they were shut in with God. They had the mark of God upon them. When you see the things that are making the world turn pale and tremble, lift up your head and rejoice, because it will soon be over. So the saints of God see these things and sigh and cry. Yet they rejoice, because they know they are saved.

> *Lord, with the signs of Your return all around me, fill me with a zeal for winning the lost to You. Amen.*

Day 68

Judgment Is Coming

Because he hath appointed a day, in the which he will judge the world in righteousness by that man whom he hath ordained.

—ACTS 17:31

JUDGMENT IS COMING. Destruction is coming. The city will be taken. They were laughed at as fools, fanatics, and enemies. They would not listen. But the saints knew that when the destruction came, the city would be taken and their business would be no good. The enemy would take everything, their houses and lands would amount to nothing. The only thing they could do was to use their money to warn the people that destruction was coming. So their money and their gold and silver and their land would not do any good. Neither will it do you any good. God help you to see it.

Blow the trumpet in Zion, sound the alarm. Jerusalem will be taken. Tribulation is coming.

The day of the Lord is near; it hasteth greatly. It is even at the door. Warn the people that they must have the seal of God on their foreheads. So we are going around getting the people saved, giving the word in the Holy Ghost that they may be sealed with the finger and mark of God in the forehead. They had to have the mark of God in their forehead to understand those things. Go through the streets of the city—note those who sigh and cry and put the mark on them—that is what God is doing today. Glory to God.

Lord Jesus, mark me as Your own and use me to sound forth the glory of Your coming. Amen.

10/21/08

Day 69

God Marks His Own

Brethren, be followers together of me, and mark them which walk so as ye have us for an example.

—PHILIPPIANS 3:17

GOD IS putting a mark on us to guard us against all the damnable things that are coming on the earth. Dear friends, don't you see. The angels are holding back the four winds. They are about to let loose. Oh, can we let loose, they are so wicked. Let the people go. No, not yet; not until we have sealed the servants of God with the seal of the Living God in their forehead. Go through the streets and put a mark upon everyone that sighs and cries. Put the mark of God on. Let them be baptized in the Holy Ghost. Jesus Christ will baptize you with the Holy Ghost and fire. He will give us wisdom, seal us with knowledge. You will not be left in the dark, but you shall know.

You who are saved and living pure holy lives

before God, if you don't get down and seek more of God and be sealed you are going to be left in the dark. If you don't get where you can feel the everlasting arms of Jesus around you, you will be carried away in the press, and you will not be ready to go up when Jesus comes. Oh, hold on until the servants of God get the light and are sealed with the seal of the Living God in their forehead.

> *Christ, I long to bear the marks of Your crucifixion to witness to Your salvation. Amen.*

Day 70

The Call of God

For many are called, but few are chosen.
— MATTHEW 22:14

So MANY prophesy this or that, and it never comes true. The prophecy was not according to the Word of God. Someone gives a person a message, and he believes God sent it, when it is not according to the Word.

When God calls you out for His Work, He will take care of you. God will give you something to eat, and He will clothe you.

There are so many who run before they are sent. It is better for them that they do not go at all. Sometimes the devil uses tongues to upset things generally. The devil can speak in tongues, and your flesh can. Be careful of the prophecy given concerning your call. Let us try the spirits and not get into the flesh.

If God doesn't call you out, don't give up

your work. Then you will have something to give. This mistake is made by many missionaries who go abroad. Some sell all they have, break up their homes, separate from their wives, and God has not called them.

> *Lord, it is Your call and Your voice I long to obey, not the voice or call of man. Amen.*

10/23/08

Day 71

A Higher Standard

*Now concerning spiritual gifts, brethren, I
would not have you ignorant.*
—1 CORINTHIANS 12:1

WHAT AILS the Pentecostal movement?
What has crept in so much? Some
people take every foolish thing for the Holy
Ghost. There are two extremes: One keeps the
Holy Ghost from working except in a certain
way; The other thinks everything is the Holy
Ghost.

One is as bad as the other. Let everything be
done by the Word of God. We are living in
the last days, and there has to be a higher standard for the Pentecostal movement. Christ is
coming. Praise His name!

*Lord Jesus, help me to live according
to the highest standard of holiness.
Amen.*

10/24/08

Day 72

The Armies of God

*And Elisha prayed ... And the Lord
opened the eyes of the young man; and he
saw: and, behold, the mountain was full
of horses and chariots of fire round about
Elisha.*

—2 KINGS 6:17

JESUS SAID they hated Him without a cause.
The real children of God are clothed with
light and power and with the Holy Ghost
from heaven, sent from the eternal throne of
God. The world does not know us, because it
did not know Him, so the devil brings all his
forces into the battle against Jesus and His
saints. But He that is in us is greater than all
that are against us. The Lord will fight our battles even if He has to bring down all the armies
of heaven.

When the prophet Elisha was surrounded
by the enemies of the Lord, his servant was
frightened because he was sure that they would
be killed. The prophet of God, however, was

calm. He looked up to God and said, "Open the young man's eyes." His eyes were opened, and he looked around. He saw the armies of the Lord with horses and chariots of fire. God sent all the artillery of heaven to surround just one prophet of God and his servant. God will do the same for us when we call upon Him.

Lord, fight my battles and be victorious in Your might. Amen.

Day 73

Stand Firm

*For as concerning this sect, we know that
every where it is spoken against.*
—ACTS 28:22

WHEN PAUL and the other apostles preached the gospel they faced great opposition. So do we. The gospel preached by the Holy Ghost with signs, stirs the devil and his hosts in these last days. They lay pits and traps to catch us as they did to our Savior at the time when they were going to throw Him over a hill to kill Him. But Jesus slipped away. The devil also hates me with a perfect hatred, and has tried many times and in many ways to kill and destroy me. I only escaped by the ever present, watchful, loving care of my Lord. He said, "Fear not, I am with you." It means everything to know that God is with us.

I have been in many places where my life was not worth a straw, but I always stood firm.

I have been in the greatest dangers, but bless and praise His holy name, He always came with the hosts of heaven, and in such a way that the fear of God fell on my enemies— whether one or a howling mob. Sometimes they could not move. Sometimes they fell like drunken men. Others ran. They were glad to escape with their lives and their liberty. In all these trials, God got the victory, for all knew that the Lord was with me, and with us, and fighting His own battles.

> *Lord, I trust You to protect me and guide me through enemy territory to the place You want me to be. Amen.*

10/26/08

Day 74

God's Protection

*There shall no evil befall thee, neither
shall any plague come nigh thy dwelling.
For he shall give his angels charge over
thee, to keep thee in all thy ways.*
—PSALMS 91:10–11

DEAR READER, we are now in the dark days,
and many who read these lines will have
to go through great danger, persecution, and
hard trials, remaining true to God. We must
stand for His Word, honor and glorify His
name, and He will protect us.

We can have faith that we will live until
Jesus comes. Claim the promise that He will
shield us from all dangers, from all the arrows
of the enemy, and from the pestilence, so that
no plague will come near us. The promises
contained in the ninety-first psalm are true for
all God's children in these last days.

Oh! Glory to His name that liveth forever
and ever, who is able to deliver His children
out of all their troubles. Then why fear when

troubles come? We must have trials to perfect us for our future home.

> *I trust You, Lord, to guard me with Your angels and to perfect me through all the trials. Amen.*

10/28/08

Dance Before the Lord

*And David danced before the Lord with
all his might.*

—2 SAMUEL 6:14

MICHAL, David's wife, did not like his
dancing. She scolded him and made
light of him. She said he was dancing before
the maidens like a lewd fellow, and made out
of his dancing as if he were base and low. But
he answered, "I was not dancing before men,
but the Lord," showing that he had lost sight
of the world and what they thought or said,
and was moved and controlled entirely by the
Holy Ghost for the Glory of God.

All the great company was blessed but
Michal. She was stricken with barrenness till
the day of her death. She sinned by making
light of the power of God in the holy dance
(just as some do today), and attributed it to
the flesh or the devil. The critics of God always

lose out, and many are in darkness till death.

The news of King David's great victory—killing the giant Goliath and destroying the great army of the Philistines—spread quickly over the land. When David returned from the slaughter, the women came out of all the cities of Israel to meet the King, singing and dancing with great joy and playing instruments of music. Now notice, in all their cities the women went out in the streets and danced with their music; men are not mentioned—just maidens. Women danced unto the Lord in honor of God, and the king, prompted by the Spirit of God, praised Him in the dance. It took courage for David to honor the King in this way, but the Lord smiled His approval by having it written by holy men of old and passed down to us in His precious Word.

> *Lord, may I be moved and controlled entirely by Your Spirit, until I lose sight of the world and praise flows from my heart in dancing. Amen.*

EVERYTHING!

10/29

Day 76

God's Power Cannot Be Bought

But Peter said unto him, Thy money perish with thee, because thou hast thought that the gift of God may be purchased with money.

—ACTS 8:20

PREACH IN a simple way, and demonstrate. The seal is put upon the word by the Holy Spirit. Many say that when we lay hands upon the people they get mesmerized. I am sorry they do not know more of the power of God. There was a great revival at Samaria. Simon the sorcerer was baptized, but none of them had been baptized with the Holy Ghost. Peter and John went to Samaria and laid hands on them, and they received the Holy Ghost.

Simon recognized the power was different from sorcery, and he wanted it. He offered them money to give him this power, that whomsoever he laid hands on might receive the Holy Ghost. The apostles were horrified. They said, "Thy money perish with thee, because thou hast thought that the gift of God can be purchased with money" (Acts 8:20).

The Holy Ghost and His power are gifts of God. No one can buy them. Many people today do not understand any more than Simon did.

By the laying on of the apostles' hands something happened: the Holy Ghost fell on those people, and they had great blessing.

> *Lord, I seek the power of the Holy Spirit not for my glory but for Yours. Amen.*

Day 77

The Power of His Resurrection

Behold, I show you a mystery; We shall
not all sleep, but we shall all be changed,
In a moment, in the twinkling of an eye,
at the last trump . . .
—1 CORINTHIANS 15:51–52

NOTHING BUT the mighty Holy Ghost will ever take you up in the clouds. He will quicken these mortal bodies; and they will be changed. We shall not have wings, but our hands and feet will be made light. Our feet shall be like "hind's feet" and we will run, skip, and almost fly. We shall know the power of the resurrection life. We shall be so filled with the Holy Ghost that our bodies will be made light. Sometimes my body is made so light, I can hardly stay.

My feet are on the earth, but my hands seem on the throne. Christ arose from the dead, and He is the resurrection and the life. People want to get the blood of Jesus over them, over their diseased bodies, in His name.

Do you believe right now? If you believe and praise the Lord in faith it shall be done. If you do not feel the joy, offer praise as a sacrifice, and ask God to give you the joy. When the unclean spirit is driven out, the disease goes, and the resurrection life comes into you.

Some dance, shout, and praise the Lord as the life of Jesus thrills through them. I declare to you on the authority of God and from my own experience, I know it is the power of God through Jesus Christ. It does not take Jesus long to do the work, but it takes some of us a long time to get there. Five minutes will do the work. Then the peace of God will flow through you like a river, and you will have joy in the Holy Ghost. As you go home, do not think about your sins. Don't commit any more sins, and don't worry about the past because it is under the blood.

Jesus, fill me with Your resurrection power. Amen.

Day 78

Pentecostal Revival

*And by the hands of the apostles were
many signs and wonders wrought among
the people; and they were all with one
accord in Solomon's porch.*

—ACTS 5:12

THIS WAS the greatest revival given in the
New Testament—greater in many ways
than Pentecost. Then they were all with one
accord and in place while awaiting the outpouring of the Spirit. You get there, and God
will shake the country.

Signs and wonders were wrought and of the
rest dare no man join himself unto them. They
were so full of fire no person dared say falsely,
"I am one of you." They were afraid God
would strike them dead.

God wants to get a people so full of His
power that others full of wildfire will say,
"God fill me with the real power."

What was the result of Pentecost? Believers
were added to the church? No, they were

added to the Lord, both men and women. Some say that this excitement and fanaticism is good enough for women, but there was also a multitude of strong-minded men there.

They brought the sick into the streets and laid them on beds and couches so that Peter's shadow might overshadow some of them. See what a cranky set they were! I wish we were just like that. Excitement rose higher and higher. The whole country was stirred. There came multitudes from the city of Jerusalem, bringing the sick, and they were healed. Why? Because they came seeking God and not man. A wonderful revival, was it not!

Lord, send Your revival to the church and to me. Amen.

Day 79

Healing and Praise

*And immediately he [the paralytic] arose,
took up the bed, and went forth before
them all; insomuch that they were all
amazed, and glorified God . . .*

—MARK 2:12

THE PARALYTIC did not break up the
meeting when he was brought to Jesus
and dropped down through the roof while
Jesus was preaching. Jesus is our example. He
was glad to have something like that happen,
because it gave Him a chance to show His
power. Jesus forgave the man all his sins and
then made him rise, take up his bed, and walk.

The people began to shout, "Glory," the
same way you do here. You cannot help it. If
you have not done it you will. A consumptive
woman was brought in here in her night robe.
I did not care what she had on—she was
healed. Hallelujah!

When the paralytic was healed, they gave
glory to God. People say today, "You never

heard such a noisy group." If they had only heard them then! We have something to make a fuss about. Dead people never make much noise, do they? There is not much noise in a graveyard!

> *Jesus I praise You for Your healing and delivering. Amen.*

r1/2/08

Day 80

Greater Works

Verily, verily, I say unto you, He that believeth on me, the works that I do shall he do also; and greater works than these shall he do; because I go unto My Father.
—JOHN 14:12

HE THAT BELIEVETH on Jesus Christ shall have such power that out of his inward parts shall flow rivers of living waters. At Pentecost, the Holy Spirit filled the apostles, and people were healed even watching for Peter's shadow.

The power of the Holy Ghost struck the sick ones and healed them, and the people marveled.

Don't you see that God works through human instrumentality? God will use us if we are swallowed up in Him.

Jesus, use me to work Your will. Amen.

Day 81

Healing and Revival

And as the lame man which was healed held Peter and John, all the people ran together unto them in the porch that is called Solomon's, and greatly wondering.

—ACTS 3:11

TAKE A PICTURE of the revival in Acts. Did they act like crazy folks? Some of the best people in Jerusalem took part in that revival. All classes of people were there. People were lying all around, getting healed, and multitudes were being saved.

It was the greatest revival, and divine healing was the drawing card. When people are healed, it does not mean simply healing, but it brings people to Christ. For example, consider the man healed at the beautiful gate of the temple.

Peter took the miracles as his text and preached. The authorities laid hands on him and commanded him not to speak or teach in the name of Jesus. But Peter and John preached in His name anyway. They prayed, and the Holy Ghost came in great power. The outgrowth of that healing in the temple was a great revival.

Lord Jesus, heal and save. Amen.

Day 82

From Whence This Power?

When they saw the boldness of Peter and John, and perceived that they were unlearned and ignorant men . . . and they took knowledge of them, that they had been with Jesus.
—ACTS 4:13

WHEN MEN AND WOMEN come in contact with this work of the Holy Ghost, hearing His words and seeing His works, there is danger lest they attribute the power present to some other agency other than the Spirit of God.

There is a danger lest they condemn the power and condemn God's servants. How often have we heard ministers say, when they heard men, women, and children speaking in other tongues, "Oh, it is the work of the devil."

Now hear what God says about that. They are speaking against the Holy Spirit. God has been working in our cities and will work in much greater measure. We expect to see greater signs and wonders. If the saints stand together as one, pray together, and shout victory together, then God will show Himself as our mighty God and Savior.

> *Lord God, as we praise You and give You glory, do signs and wonders in our midst that others may come to Christ as Savior. Amen.*

2008, Nov 4 – Election Day

What ever happens, I believe You will use the results to bring others to the knowledge of You. For me, it wasn't about voting for the winning man, it was voting/standing for Your principles + values — no matter what.

Day 83

If We Do Not Have Power

And with great power gave the apostles witness of the resurrection of the Lord Jesus: and great grace was upon them all.
—ACTS 4:33

IF WE haven't the power, let us confess it and ask God to give us the power He first gave the disciples. If those who come to the Lord will be filled as they were on the day of Pentecost, we will have streams of living water rushing through us and flowing to the very ends of the earth. Jesus Christ was baptized in the Holy Ghost. But He did not have all power until He had finished His course. He could have turned away from the cross, but He went all the way, and cried out, "It is finished." His last act was going down into death.

But God Almighty raised Him up, and when He came up all power was given Him— all power! He sent His disciples out in His name and said that those who believed on Him should cast out devils, speak in new tongues, lay hands on the sick, and if they drank any deadly thing (accidentally, of course) it would not hurt them. He said to the disciples, "Verily, verily, I say unto you, he that believeth on me, the works that I do shall he do also; and greater works than these shall he do; because I go unto my Father" (John 14:12).

When Pentecost came they were all in the upper room, waiting. They were all saved, pure, and in one accord—no divisions, no controversy. They did not know how the "promise of the Father" was going to come, but they were waiting for it. Suddenly, the Spirit, as a cyclone, came and filled the whole building. A great tidal wave of power was turned upon them, and they were all filled with living water.

Lord, fill me with the same power as You did those early disciples so that Your tidal wave of power may sweep over me. Amen.

Day 84

Christ Is Preparing His Bride

I am my beloved's, and my beloved is mine.

—SONG OF SOLOMON 6:3

THE KING of glory will be married to His bride. Don't you know that every good thing the world enjoys, God is going to let us enjoy ten-thousand-fold? There will be the greatest banquet, the most wonderful occasion ever heard of, when we shall eat bread and drink wine in the kingdom. The bride is now in training. The Holy Ghost is the dove. The singing is the cooing of the dove before the storm.

Did you ever hear the doves before the storm, call to their mates to seek shelter? So the Holy Ghost is cooing and chirping, calling us to seek shelter from the tribulation storms that are coming upon the earth. The Lord has us in training, making our bodies light and supple so that we can go up.

May the Lord help us to be filled with the Holy Ghost so that we can rise. It is the only moving power in the church of Christ, His mighty agent. He wants us to carry on His business through His body. Let us get the fire from heaven that will enable us to do business for God, and be careful that we do not attribute the power of God to the devil, lest we commit the unpardonable sin.

Jesus, You are my beloved, my first love, and I eagerly await the time when You come for Your bride. Amen.

Day 85

Women and the Gospel

*Now upon the first day of the week . . .
they* [the women] *came unto the sepulcher . . . And they entered in, and found
not the body of the Lord Jesus.*

—LUKE 24:1, 3

WOMEN WERE called and commissioned
by the angel sent from heaven, and by
the Lord Jesus Christ, to preach the gospel
(Matt. 28:5–10).

The cowardly disciples had forsaken the
Savior and fled. Peter denied the Savior and
swore that he never knew him, but many
women followed Him and stood by the cross.
They went on to the sepulcher and saw the
body laid away with a great stone door over
the tomb. (Matt. 27:55–61).

These women went home sad and broken-
hearted. They spent the night in preparing to
embalm the body of their Lord. Then they
returned to pay a last tribute to a dear friend.
They came to the tomb on the first day of the

week. The grave was empty. The Lord was not there. The women were the first to witness the resurrected Lord and to be commissioned to proclaim the gospel.

Observe the wonderful mission that Jesus had entrusted to these weak women: they were to preach the first resurrection sermon and to risk their lives gathering together the followers of Christ. God is calling women today all over the world to work in various places in the vineyard and proclaim that He is risen.

Lord, mightily use women to declare Your resurrection to the world. Amen.

Day 86

Handmaidens Will Prophesy

*And on my servants and on my hand-
maidens I will pour out in those days of
my Spirit; and they shall prophesy.*
—ACTS 2:18

GOD IS promising great blessings and power
to qualify His handmaidens for the last
great harvest just before the notable day of the
Lord comes. We must first be baptized into
Christ by one Spirit, that is to be born of the
Spirit. Then we ought to be anointed with
power and wisdom. The Spirit ought to be
poured out like oil on our heads, to give us
knowledge of the deep things of God. The
Lord says women shall prophesy, and He has
promised this greatest gift to his handmaidens
and daughters.

*Lord, help us to hear Your prophetic
message through Your daughters and
handmaidens. Amen.*

11/9/08

Day 87

The Woman Evangelist

*And many of the Samaritans of that city
believed on him [Jesus] for the saying of
the woman which testifieth, He told me
all that ever I did.*

—JOHN 4:39

WHILE JESUS sat at Jacob's well to rest, a poor woman, one who was living in sin, came to the well to get water. She had fallen very low and was despised by her friends, so that she had no one to lift her up and tell her of a better way. But Jesus came to seek the lost—to seek her and lift her up.

God help us to follow this example. If sinners feel like their feet are slipping into the pit of hell, Jesus is the mighty Savior. He can lift them up and make them children of the King.

Jesus preached salvation. The Samaritan woman at the well was converted. Then she left her pitcher and took the well of salvation with her. Running into the city, she went up one street and down another with her face aglow with God's glory. There was a great revival there at the well through this woman. This was the result of one sermon by a weak woman. Many were converted by the preaching of the woman, who said, "He told me all the things that I ever did."

Lord, use women to win many to You.
Amen.

11/10/08

Day 88

Weep for the Lost

*Blessed are they that mourn: for they shall
be comforted.*

—MATTHEW 5:4

IF WE WEEP and mourn on account of poor
sinners, we shall laugh through all eternity. Oh, let us work now, and by and by our
weeping will be over. We shall come rejoicing,
bringing in the sheaves. We can say, "Here am
I, Father, and the children thou hast given me."

A child was dying. "Father," said she, "I
have come to the river and am waiting for the
ferrymen to take me over."

"Does it seem dark and cold, my child?"

"Oh, no, there is no darkness here. The
river is covered with solid silver. The boats,
they are solid light. I am not afraid of the
ferrymen. Oh, I see over the river! There is a
great and beautiful city, all filled with light.
The angels are making music. Oh, I see the

168

most beautiful blessed Jesus. He has taken me in His bosom."

And thus she passes over the river of death, made like a silver stream by the presence of her Redeemer.

> *Lord, help me to weep for the lost.*
> *Amen.*

Day 89

God's Vision

Blessed are the pure in heart: for they shall see God.

—MATTHEW 5:8

THE WAYS and wisdom of God are foolishness to the unsaved, but God hath revealed them to his chosen ones; yea the deep things of God. Oh, praise the Lord for the wisdom, knowledge, fellowship, and presence of the Lord who lives and walks with us continually.

Stephen was not an apostle, but he was full of faith and the Holy Ghost, and we all are commanded to be filled with the same power. He did great miracles among the people. When he so nobly defended the risen Christ, fearless of losing his life, his false accusers looked on his face and said it looked like the face of an angel.

The pure gospel, accompanied by the power

of the Holy Ghost, cut them to the heart.
They would not accept it, and they gnashed
upon him with their teeth (Acts 7:54–56).

But Stephen, filled with the Holy Ghost,
looked up and saw heaven. He saw Jesus
standing at the right hand of God's throne. He
had a pure heart that saw God.

Saul had no vision of Christ. Yes, he was
one of the best scholars of his day, and had a
polished form of religion, but he would not
believe Stephen's vision. Saul simply stood there
watching the stoning of Stephen. Visions, or
visible demonstrations of the power of God
could not be accepted by the scholar, only by
the one filled with the Spirit. We need God's
wisdom, not man's knowledge, to see His
dreams and visions.

*Lord, show me Your dreams and
visions. Amen.*

Kill me, so I can see You alive.

11/12/08

Day 90

The Need for Visions

Where there is no vision, the people perish.

—Proverbs 29:18

THE BOOK OF REVELATION is the most wonderful of all in the Bible. Christ appeared to John in person and gave him one vision after another. He showed him the heavenly city, the great city of gold with its jasper walls. John was told about the climate, the inhabitants, the size, and all that happened there. He had visions of the great judgment day, of the lake of fire and brimstone, and all the lost that were swept into it. The Lord told John to write all that he saw and heard, and to show it to the churches.

The prophet said that the time would come when, if anyone had a vision, they would be ashamed to tell it. That time is here. The masses of church leaders look upon everything

supernatural as a disgrace and cry out, "Hypnotism, excitement, emotionalism, and drunkenness." Just like the religious Jews of Jesus' day, they are filled with a dead form of religion.

The churches are filled with unconverted people. Where there are no visions, the people perish. If there is not power enough for visions, there is not enough to save a soul.

> *Lord, help the church see the visions You give. Amen.*